7 Steps to Becoming FINANCIALLY Free

PHIL LENAHAN

7 Steps to Becoming FINANCIALLY Free

A Catholic Guide to Managing Your Money

OUR SUNDAY VISITOR PUBLISHING DIVISION
OUR SUNDAY VISITOR, INC.
HUNTINGTON, IN 46750

Dedication

nyone who writes a book knows of the commitment involved. What often goes unnoticed is the commitment required from those closest to the author, and that has certainly been true in the case of this project. I'd like to dedicate this book to my beautiful wife, Chelsey, and our children. Thanks for your patience, your support, and the time you took to listen to ideas and read through many rough drafts. I love you all!

CONTENTS

PART II. ACHIEVING FINANCIAL FREEDOM

Acknowledgments

ooks don't come together on their own. I'd like to thank my friends at Our Sunday Visitor for believing in this project and for their valuable input. Greg Erlandson, Beth McNamara, John Christensen, and the staff at Our Sunday Visitor have all had a hand in guiding this work through to completion. I'd also like to give special thanks to Jackie Lindsey and Katie Hammerling for their invaluable assistance during the editing process. Finally, I'm not sure the project ever would have gotten underway without the encouragement of my friends Bill and Mary Lou Piatkiewicz.

7 STEPS TO BECOMING FINANCIALLY FREE

 STEP ONE   Be a "Steward of Providence"

 STEP TWO   Assess Where You Are – Develop a Plan

 STEP THREE $2,000 Emergency Savings

 STEP FOUR   Eliminate Debt – Accelerate It!

 STEP FIVE   Rainy-Day Fund – Six Months' Expenses

 STEP SIX   Review Insurance and Estate Planning Needs

 STEP SEVEN   Save and Invest with a Purpose

WHY TALK ABOUT MONEY?

REAL PEOPLE, REAL ISSUES

*B*efore I started writing *7 Steps to Becoming Financially Free*, I really began to take notice of just how many books, magazines, and other sources of information there are available on money management and how they're all loaded with techniques for achieving wealth and "having it all." It made me wonder: Is there really a need for another one?

What sets this guide apart is that while it is about managing money, its primary aim is to show the important link that exists between our faith journey and how we handle our money. My background as a certified public accountant and years of experience with counseling couples and individuals with their budgets and goals convinced me that there's a great need for a guide on what it means to be *truly* financially free, how to achieve that sense of freedom, and how to enjoy the peace that comes with it.

One of the couples that really inspired me to pen this book was Paul and Ann, the parents of four beautiful children. I'd seen them at church before, but I hadn't had the chance to get to know them until they asked if I could counsel them on money management.

During our first meeting, I listened as they summarized the problems they were having. On the surface, it was pretty typical stuff — you know the story: there was always a little too much "month" left at the end of the money. About $10,000 in credit card debt had accumulated over a few years, and they had no savings. Their conclusion? "We just don't make enough money."

As we spoke a bit more, Paul and Ann admitted they had no budget — and therefore no road map to direct how they spent their money. They just lived paycheck to paycheck, and when "surprises" occurred, they put the extras on credit cards. For a long time they could handle the minimum balance, so they just put off creating a real solution to the overspending problem. Now even paying the minimum was becoming a challenge, and this was the ultimate catalyst for setting up our visit. I assigned them some reading and asked them to complete an initial budget, and we set a follow-up appointment for a week later.

Now we were meeting for the second time. As I sat across the table from them, tension filled the room. Paul was pointing out all the areas where he felt Ann was overspending: too many new clothes and shoes. According to him, her shopping was the reason for their problems. With a sense of defensiveness, Ann shot back that Paul funneled an awful lot of money toward his antique-car hobby. I felt as if I was in the middle of a war zone with bullets flying! Even more disappointing was the knowledge that these bullets were hitting their mark. The visit came to a close, and I never heard from Paul and Ann again. Later I found out that they'd divorced.

When I volunteered to counsel people who came to our pastor with financial difficulties, I didn't realize that the discussions would involve much more than finances. But because money touches so many aspects of our lives — the relationships between husband and wife, parents and children, spouses and in-laws; our work; and, most importantly, our faith — I found myself providing counsel on these issues as well.

Unfortunately, Paul and Ann aren't anomalies. Money problems impact many in our society, including college students who get in over their heads with student loans and credit cards; young couples who use credit to pay for their weddings, honeymoons, and home-furnishing expenses; and folks who tap into the equity in their houses to cover habitual overspending — even if it's for vacations and toys. It's especially tragic, as with Paul and Ann, when something as sacred as a marriage or family is damaged to the point where two people see no alternative but divorce.

Even our government has a difficult time managing its financial affairs. There are deficits forecast as far as the eye can see! Yet it's quite amusing to hear so many people criticize the government's overspending when they don't have a handle on their own. Don't get me wrong: The government should have the discipline to live within its means. But our representatives are by-products of the same culture as the rest of us, so it seems odd to expect more from them than we do from ourselves. When it's so common that a husband and wife can't agree on financial priorities for their family, why should we imagine that the 535 members of Congress will do any better? Especially when they have the authority to levy taxes and print extra money!

I remember my dad sharing many stories of life during the Depression. He spoke of how families pulled together out of necessity and how important it was to set spending priorities — because if you didn't, you weren't going to have enough to cover the basics of food and shelter. Now, instead of developing the habit of saving for a rainy day, we're taught by the consumer culture to buy all that we want (and more) when we want it, without concern for the cost or how we'll pay for it. If we don't have the money today... well, that's what credit cards and home equity loans are for, right?

While none of us would wish for another nationwide depression, I can tell you that many a family is experiencing its own personal financial crash. Here are some statistics that provide a snapshot of just how poorly we're doing as a culture at managing our financial affairs:

Startling Statistics

- The average American household has about 8 major bank credit cards (17 when you include department store and gas cards) that carry a combined balance of almost $8,000.[1]
- More than 19 million households, or about 17 percent of American families, make only minimum payments on their cards.[2]
- There were nearly 1.6 million bankruptcy filings in 2004, compared to less than 400,000 in 1986.[3]
- More than 50 percent of Americans are worried about not having enough money for retirement.[4]

- Charitable giving averages 1.7 percent of household income for all Americans and about 1 percent for American Catholics.[5]
- Fifty-one percent of *Christians* believe money is the main symbol of success in life.[6]
- Fifty percent of all marriages end in divorce, and money issues are pointed to as a significant cause of many breakups.[7]

These statistics certainly seem hard to believe, but after counseling countless families who struggle day in and day out with their finances, I'm not surprised. The most alarming fact is that the majority of couples obtaining a divorce state that one of their primary conflicts is money. This shows how explosive financial problems are and how much human damage they can do.

GOD'S PLAN FOR YOUR FINANCES

When most people think about what it takes to successfully manage their money, what comes to mind are budgets, checkbook management, reconciling of bank accounts, monitoring of investments, and tax planning, among other things. Sure, these are all important, and this book will help you manage these tasks, but there's something even more crucial: The *attitude* you have toward money will do more for determining whether you become truly financially free than any other issue. In fact, I believe that people's attitudes represent 90 percent of the reason they either succeed or fail with their finances.

What do I mean by attitude? It starts with the role money plays in your life. Is it a means of fulfilling your God-given responsibilities, or is it an end in itself? Are your financial goals determined by the culture, with an emphasis on having? Or do they have as their foundation the sure-footed principles we find in sacred Scripture and the teaching Tradition of our Catholic faith, which emphasizes "being" over "having"?

The way you can achieve true financial freedom and peace is to recognize that *God has a plan for your life — including your finances.* He is our Father and wants what's best for us. Our faith provides the answers we're looking for, so we can develop a healthy, wholesome, and holy attitude when it comes to how we manage our money. In fact, how you handle your money is one of the best indicators of the strength and vitality of your spiritual life. The Bible teaches about money on two levels. Many Bible references deal with principles that guide our attitude toward money. These recognize an inherent tension that exists between our attitude toward money and our relationship with God. They help us place money in its proper perspective so that we can grow closer to the Lord. Other references, especially from the book of Proverbs, provide plenty of very practical guidelines for daily living.

For too long we've allowed a wall to separate our faith lives from our money. It's time we break down that barrier and move forward on the journey to true financial freedom: freedom from debt, learning to be generous, and knowing how to set godly priorities, which includes saving for the important things in life.

ARE YOU READY FOR *TRUE* FINANCIAL FREEDOM?

Each of us will find both strengths and weaknesses as we examine how we relate to money from an interior perspective. Most people uncover an area that's a particular challenge, and we can call this a "predominant" fault or tendency. Such faults require extra effort to overcome, yet we often see that making such an effort leads to a great deal of personal and spiritual growth. In fact, this is what helps us become better people — people who more closely imitate Christ as we apply the virtues to how we handle our money.

There are many stages to our lives, with varied financial implications along the way. My purpose in writing this book has been to help you bring balance and peace into your financial life, no matter what stage you find yourself in. Maybe you are engaged to be married and want to get off on the right foot. Or you might be raising a young family and find yourself with increasing debts and no sense of how to develop a "financial roadmap" for your future. Maybe you've been pursuing "success" in your career to the exclusion of your relationships with your spouse and children — and especially the Lord.

In this book, the path to true financial freedom and peace has been marked out for you. Here's what you can expect to learn along the way:

- What Christ and his Church have to say about handling money, and what that means for you (Step One).
- How to strengthen your marriage and family life, and how to teach your children the ABCs of managing their resources wisely (Step One).
- What it means to have "work with a purpose," and how it applies to you (Step One).
- The tools you need to create a budget — and stick to it — and to keep all your financial affairs organized (Step Two).
- The basics of saving and investing, and what you need to know to properly plan for your and your children's future (Step Three, Step Five, and Step Seven).
- How you can break free from the bondage of debt (Step Four).
- Answers to your questions about buying and owning your home and smart tips on how to become mortgage free (Step Four).
- How to manage risks to you and your family through the appropriate use of insurance (Step Six).
- Why it's important to put in place basic estate planning mechanisms for the well-being of your family (Step Six).

In conclusion, if I had the opportunity to write a personal letter to those wanting to achieve a sense of balance and peace with their finances, here's what I'd say:

Dear friend,

Over the years, I've had the opportunity to visit with thousands of people regarding their financial situations. A recurring theme that is mentioned is the feeling of being in bondage. When one hears of financial bondage, they often think of problems associated with credit card debt and other forms of consumer credit. It is true that many people in our society are slaves to debt.

But financial bondage takes many forms. It occurs when spouses fail to communicate about money issues, leading to a lack of unity in the marriage. It occurs when someone becomes a workaholic, or when one seeks satisfaction in acquiring "stuff." In both cases, relationships with God and family are often relegated to the back seat.

Financial bondage occurs when no provision is made for retirement years. It occurs when our children fail to learn the important values that our faith imparts about the importance of being a good steward, and they find themselves making financial mistakes in their early adult years that can take a lifetime to resolve.

Most Americans experience some form of financial bondage, so it's important to know that you're not alone. But that doesn't mean you should stay there. Our Lord wants so much more for us. He wants us to experience the peace and contentment that come from being truly financially free.

How can we achieve that freedom and what does it mean for you? We achieve true financial freedom by learning and applying godly principles to our financial affairs. These principles are found in the Bible — God's love letter to us — and the teaching of our Catholic faith. By applying these principles consistently, you'll find your marriage and parenting skills enhanced, your debt eliminated, an ability to save for future needs, and a joy that comes with learning to be generous.

The journey toward true financial freedom is simple, but you'll need to do your part. *No one can do this for you.* It's up to you to make the commitment to be a good steward of the gifts God has given you. It's a privilege for me to be walking with you. Shall we get started?

With warmest regards,
Phil

Part

I

FAITH AND FINANCES

Chapter 1

FAITH-DRIVEN GOALS: GOD'S CALL

*T*here was once a stingy lawyer who was diagnosed with a terminal illness. He was determined to prove wrong the saying "You can't take it with you." After much thought and consideration, the old ambulance-chaser finally figured out how to take at least *some* of his money with him when he died.

He instructed his wife to go to the bank and withdraw enough cash to fill two pillow cases. He then asked her to take them to the attic and leave them in a space directly above his bed. His plan was that when he passed away, he'd reach out and grab the money on his way to heaven.

Several weeks after the funeral, the deceased lawyer's wife was cleaning up in the attic when she came upon the two stuffed pillow cases. "Oh, that darned fool!" she exclaimed. "I knew he should have had me put the money in the basement!"

Now I don't mean to pick on lawyers — I've worked closely with one for many years! But this story does remind us that when we're called home by the Lord, we'll be leaving our material possessions behind. Paul says in 1 Timothy 6:7, "For we brought nothing into the world, and we cannot take anything out of the world." Yet for many of us, life seems to be largely driven by an endless pursuit of these same possessions we'll be leaving behind. How ironic that is!

I remember reading the final testament of Pope John Paul II after he passed away. I was struck by one of the sentences that read, "I leave no property behind me of which it is necessary to dispose." What a simple yet profound statement. It reminds me of Job, who said, "Naked I came from my mother's womb, and naked shall I return; the LORD gave, and the LORD has taken away; blessed be the name of the LORD" (Job 1:21).

While those of us with families aren't often called to the complete level of physical detachment that John Paul II demonstrated, we are expected to achieve a sense of detachment from the gifts God has given us so our love can be properly reserved for him and for others. As I mentioned in the introduction, there is an important link between our faith journey and how we handle our money. This link begins with a discussion of what really matters in life, and the things we often overlook in the daily hubbub of activity that surrounds our homes and workplaces. We need to ask ourselves the following questions:

- What comes after my short life on earth?
- Does how I live today have an impact on my eternal destiny?
- Where can I receive the help and guidance I need during this life so I can spend eternity with Jesus?
- What role does the managing of my money have on my relationship with Christ?
- What does it mean to be truly financially free?

PLANNING FOR ETERNITY

It's important for our financial objectives to support our goals for life, and there's really one objective we should have that surpasses all others, one that relates to the bigger picture: As Christians, we must always keep in mind the reason for our existence. Remember Jesus' words: "For what does it profit a man, to gain the whole world and forfeit his life?" (Mark 8:36).

The *Catechism of the Catholic Church* opens by quoting the following verse of the gospel of John: ". . . this is eternal life, that they know thee the only true God, and Jesus Christ, whom thou hast sent" (Jn 17:3). And the very first section of the *Catechism* is titled "The Life of Man — to Know and Love God." That is our purpose!

During Jesus' time on earth, he taught about the important things in life. He spoke of his relationship with the Father and the Holy Spirit and how we can share eternal life with them. When he spoke of money or material things (and he did so frequently), it was often in the form of parables that emphasized how possessions can easily be an obstacle to what our main goal in life should be: to spend eternity with God.

I remember vividly the time of my father's passing. His health had been failing for a few years and had begun a more precipitous decline. My family and I were fortunate to be able to care for him in the home he had lived in for many years, which was also the home we were raised in. A few weeks before his death, it became apparent that his time with us here was coming to a close.

All the family gathered at the house for that last week. It was a very special time as we had the chance to visit with Dad and with one another, reminiscing about our early years. I was especially struck at how, during these last few days, life slowed down dramatically and our entire focus turned to our relationships in the family — especially with our father. Sitting with Dad, I'd notice him folding his hands in quiet prayer. Then he'd open his gentle blue eyes and we'd visit for a bit.

Why do I mention my dad's final days on earth? Because through this experience I learned firsthand how, when we reach the final stages of our lives, we're not going to be worried about our bank accounts or investments. We're going to be focused on the people we love and on preparing ourselves to meet our Creator. Psalm 39:4–6 says, "LORD, let me know my end, and what is the measure of my days; let me know how fleeting my life is! Behold, thou hast made my days a few handbreaths, and my lifetime is as nothing in thy sight. Surely every man stands as a mere breath! Surely man goes about as a shadow! Surely for nought are they in turmoil; man heaps up, and knows not who will gather!"

We also need to remember that we will be judged by our Lord upon our death. Paul writes, "For we shall all stand before the judgment seat of God. . . . So each of us shall give account of himself to God" (Rom 14:10, 12). All of our thoughts, words, and deeds are known by God and will be judged by him. Ecclesiastes 12:14 says, "For God will bring every deed into judgment, with every secret thing, whether good or evil."

The *Catechism* speaks of our particular judgment: "Each man receives his eternal retribution in his immortal soul at the very moment of his death, in a particular judgment that refers his life to Christ: either entrance into the blessedness of heaven — through a purification or immediately — or immediate and everlasting damnation."[8] Our lives need to be lived with that in mind.

I remember hearing Dr. James Dobson, the founder of Focus on the Family, on his radio show one day. He was sharing a special moment he had with his children, when he was letting them know that the only thing really important to him was that he'd see them on "the other side." He was pleading with them to live their lives for Christ. That pretty much keeps it in perspective, doesn't it? Most of us have known people who died suddenly, without any time to prepare for their particular judgments. Now is the time to be right with God!

Often, our lives are so full of competing demands for our time and resources that we lose sight of the fact that life on earth is short and the life to come is eternal. 2 Peter 3:10–11 reminds us, "But the day of the Lord will come like a thief, and then the heavens will pass away with a loud noise, and the elements will be dissolved with fire, and the earth and the works that are upon it will be burned up. Since all these things are thus to be dissolved, what sort of persons ought you to be in lives of holiness and godliness . . ."

So as we set financial goals that will lead to true freedom, the reality of eternity must be kept front and center. We want to be able to say, like Paul, "I have fought the good fight, I have finished the race, I have kept the faith. Henceforth there is laid up for me the crown of righteousness, which the Lord, the righteous judge, will award to me on that day" (2 Tim 4:7–8).

CALL TO HOLINESS

God loves us so much that he gave us his Son, who redeemed us by dying on the cross. God wants us to imitate Christ's sacrificial love so that we can enjoy eternal life with him. We're each called to a life of personal holiness, and Jesus gives us our marching orders when he says, "Be perfect, as your heavenly Father is perfect" (Mt 5:48).

How is it possible to "be perfect" as Christ is asking? We know that on our own we can't do it, but we also know that with God's grace, all things are possible. "In order to reach this perfection, the faithful should use the strength dealt out to them by Christ's gift, so that . . . doing the will of the Father in everything, they may wholeheartedly devote themselves to the glory of God and to the service of their neighbor" (*LG* 40 § 2).[9]

Just as Jesus went through the Passion on Good Friday before rising on Easter Sunday, we're reminded that "the way of perfection passes by way of the cross. There is no holiness without renunciation and spiritual battle. Spiritual progress entails the ascesis and mortification that gradually lead to living in the peace and joy of the Beatitudes."[10]

Our true goal in life is to be holy, which is the perfection of charity.[11] And how do we know what it means to be holy and to love perfectly? We look to Jesus, to his example and teaching. "The Word became flesh *to be our model of holiness.*"[12]

Jesus' teaching was at the same time simple and profound. How are we called to love? He tells us, "If you love me, you will keep my commandments" (Jn 14:15). What are those commandments? When asked which commandment is the greatest, Jesus said, "You shall love the Lord your God with all your heart, and with all your soul, and with all your mind. This is the great and first commandment. And a second is like it. You shall love your neighbor as yourself" (Mt 22:37–39).

I remember being in Toronto with two of my children for World Youth Day in 2002. Pope John Paul II asked the youths to be "people of the Beatitudes." The Beatitudes are found in Jesus' Sermon on the Mount (Mt 5:3–11) and are one of the most beautiful passages in Scripture. They guide us to a better understanding of what it means to love perfectly. "Jesus is the model for the Beatitudes and the norm of the new law: 'Love one another as I have loved you' (Jn 15:12)."[13]

The Beatitudes

Blessed are the poor in spirit, for theirs is the kingdom of heaven.

Blessed are those who mourn, for they shall be comforted.

Blessed are the meek, for they shall inherit the earth.

Blessed are those who hunger and thirst for righteousness, for they shall be satisfied.

Blessed are the merciful, for they shall obtain mercy.

Blessed are the pure in heart, for they shall see God.

Blessed are the peacemakers, for they shall be called sons of God.

Blessed are those who are persecuted for righteousness' sake, for theirs is the kingdom of heaven.

Blessed are you when men revile you and persecute you and utter all kinds of evil against you falsely on my account. Rejoice and be glad, for your reward is great in heaven, for so men persecuted the prophets who were before you.

So that's God's call to us — to learn how to love! It's up to us to cooperate with the grace God gives us so that we will respond generously and wholeheartedly to that call.

HOLINESS AND FINANCIAL FREEDOM

You might say, "Well fine, Phil, my relationship with God is important to me, and I do want to grow in Christian love. But how is that going to help me establish financial goals?" Growing in your relationship with Christ and being faithful to him and his teachings should be your number one goal in life, and it should be your first financial goal as well! All the other financial goals and priorities you set will flow from your decision to be faithful to Christ.

Remember, Jesus spoke often of money and possessions. There are over 1,000 references to money and material things in sacred Scripture and a wealth of guidance provided through the magisterial teaching of the Church. The fact that Jesus said so much about money should matter to us, and it's important for us to listen and act on his words. These teachings provide principles that can effectively guide our financial decision making with respect to:

- marriage and money,
- children and money,
- the importance of having a financial plan,

- being free from debt and avoiding cosigning,
- giving,
- saving and investing,
- spending,
- work and earning money.

These teachings give us confidence in what the Lord wants for us and from us, and they will lead us to financial freedom. Jesus tells us in Matthew 7:24–27, "Every one then who hears these words of mine and does them will be like a wise man who built his house upon the rock; and the rain fell, and the floods came, and the winds blew and beat upon that house, but it did not fall, because it had been founded on the rock. And every one who hears these words of mine and does not do them will be like a foolish man who built his house on the sand; and the rain fell, and the floods came, and the winds blew and beat against that house, and it fell; and great was the fall of it."

So let us accept Jesus' call to be like the wise man. He has shown us the way. It's up to us to follow him. Remember what the Blessed Mother said at the wedding in Cana: "Do whatever he tells you" (Jn 2:5). True love requires no less!

ALL THAT WE HAVE BELONGS TO GOD

From the vantage point of eternity, the most important financial decision you'll make during your lifetime will be to recognize that all you have comes from God and that he is sovereign over all things.

We read in Deuteronomy 10:14, "Behold, to the LORD your God belong heaven and the heaven of the heavens, the earth with all that is in it." This theme of God's ownership is repeated in 1 Chronicles 29:11: "Thine, O LORD, is the greatness, and the power, and the glory, and the victory, and the majesty; for all that is in the heavens and in the earth is thine; thine is the kingdom, O LORD, and thou art exalted as head above all."

And yet God in his sovereignty has chosen to collaborate with man. He entrusts us with the use of resources and asks us to manage them in ways that are pleasing to him. "In the beginning God entrusted the earth and its resources to the common stewardship of mankind to take care of them, master them by labor, and enjoy their fruits."[14]

In the United States, we have a strong sense of the right to private property, and the Church certainly upholds that right. Still, we need to remember that the acquisition of private property cannot be our ultimate goal. The *Catechism* sums it up best when it says:

> The *right to private property*, acquired or received in a just way, does not do away with the original gift of the earth to the whole of mankind. The *universal destination of goods* remains primordial, even if the promotion of the common good requires respect for the right to private property and its exercise.
>
> "In his use of things man should regard the external goods he legitimately owns not merely as exclusive to himself but common to others also, in the sense that they can benefit others as well as himself" (GS 69 § 1). The ownership of any property makes its holder a **steward of Providence**, with the task of making it fruitful and communicating its benefits to others, first of all his family.[15]

When we recognize that God is sovereign over all that we have and accept the role of steward, we find that our attitude toward money changes. Instead of the self-seeking that is so prevalent in our society and leads many people into financial and spiritual straits, we use the gifts we have been given for the well-being of our family, those close to us, and for the greater good of mankind.

GOD AS TRUSTED FATHER

In addition to recognizing that all we have ultimately belongs to God, another important aspect of transforming our attitude toward money comes with learning to trust God as our Father and provider. In the Sermon on the Mount, our Lord says, "Therefore, do not be anxious, saying, 'What shall we eat?' or 'What shall we wear?' For the Gentiles seek all these things; and your heavenly father knows that you need them all. But seek first his kingdom and his righteousness, and all these things shall be yours as well" (Mt 6:31–33).

A key phrase in this passage is "heavenly Father." We have a Father in heaven who loves us so much that he gave his only Son for our redemption. His desire is for us to trust completely in him as beloved children.

Our society has made incredible advances in science and technology over the last several decades, and these are good when used in ways consistent with God's plan. However, one drawback is that we can begin to believe that we're in control of everything and, as a result, forget to trust in God. The Second Vatican Council put it this way: "Today, however, especially with the help of science and technology, he [man] has extended his mastery over nearly the whole of nature and continues to do so.... Hence many benefits once looked for, especially from heavenly powers, man has now enterprisingly procured for himself."[16]

It's easy to see how this issue of control can influence our attitude toward money. We begin to believe that we're in complete control and are no longer dependent upon God for our daily sustenance. We can also forget to give thanks daily for his provision.

One of the great accounts of divine providence in the Old Testament is the story of Elijah and the widow:

> And after a while the brook dried up, because there was no rain in the land.
>
> Then the word of the LORD came to him. "Arise, go to Zarephath, which belongs to Sidon, and dwell there. Behold, I have commanded a widow there to feed you." So he arose and went to Zarephath; and when he came to the gate of the city, behold, a widow was there gathering sticks; and he called to her and said, "Bring me a little water in a vessel, that I may drink." And as she was going to bring it, he called to her and said, "Bring me a morsel of bread in your hand." And she said, "As the LORD your God lives, I have nothing baked, only a handful of meal in a jar, and a little oil in a cruse; and now, I am gathering a couple of sticks, that I may go in and prepare it for myself and my son, that

we may eat it, and die." And Elijah said to her, "Fear not; go and do as you have said; but first make me a little cake of it and bring it to me, and afterward make for yourself and your son. For thus says the LORD the God of Israel, 'The jar of meal shall not be spent, and the cruse of oil shall not fail, until the day that the LORD sends rain upon the earth.'" And she went and did as Elijah said; and she, and he, and her household ate for many days. The jar of meal was not spent, neither did the cruse of oil fail, according to the word of the LORD which he spoke by Elijah (1 Kings 17:7–16).

What heroic faith this widow had. We're called to this same faith, knowing that our heavenly Father will provide for our needs. In the next chapter, I'll show you how changing your attitude from ownership to stewardship can revolutionize the way you handle money and set you free from financial bondage.

 FREEDOM DIVIDENDS

- Strive to be a man or woman of the Beatitudes. Memorize them.
- Pray for a docile heart that seeks to do God's will rather than seeking your own desires.

Chapter 2

FAITH-DRIVEN GOALS: OUR RESPONSE

A teenage girl was sharing her hopes and dreams for the future with her parish priest. She said she wanted to do well on the college entrance exams, and the priest nodded and asked, "Then what?" She spoke of going to a prestigious college in order to get into a high-paying career. The priest nodded again and said, "Then what?" She told him that she was going to make a lot of money so she could buy whatever she wanted and be happy. The priest responded, "Then what?"

Eventually, the priest's gentle probing got the teenager thinking about her later years and eventual death. He wanted to get the young woman to look at the bigger picture — the issue of eternity that we covered in the last chapter — and realize that ultimate happiness can't be found in what we possess.

Just as with this young teen, we all need to answer the "then what?" question. We're all in a spiritual battle, and how we handle our money and the other gifts God has given us is an important part of that struggle. Now, I don't want anyone to think that having the goal of a solid education, a good career, or owning a nice home to raise a family in are wrong. But if we go about setting financial goals apart from our relationship with the Lord, we'll find that our desire for *things* will outstrip our desire for *God*. The *Catechism of the Catholic Church* reminds us that "our thirst for another's goods is immense, infinite, never quenched" (*Roman Catechism*, III, 37; cf. Sir 5:8).[17] This thirst, unless tempered by a close walk with the Lord, often leads to overspending and debt problems that wreak havoc on family life, causing a downward spiral.

John Paul II often spoke of how we have become a society of "having" rather than a society of "being." He continually called us to the fully human life we're destined for. We need to grow in our understanding of what God wants for us rather than pursuing what *we* want. "For my thoughts are not your thoughts, neither are your ways my ways, says the LORD. For as the heavens are higher than the earth, so are my ways higher than your ways and my thoughts than your thoughts" (Is 55:8–9).

WHAT'S YOUR MONEY PERSONALITY TYPE?

Whether we like it or not, much of our lives revolve around money. And as we consider how God calls us to act with respect to our finances, it's important for us to recognize that how we handle money really is a function of who we are. This includes our core personality traits and our life experiences.

I've taught many people about applying God's principles to their finances, and over the years I've noticed that there are a number of "personality types" when it comes to managing money. Most of us can relate to a few of the profiles, yet one will tend to be predominant. Understanding which personality type best fits us is important, since it has an impact on how we relate to God and others when it comes to money matters.

By design, the following caricatures take these attitudes to extreme levels, so don't feel that there has to be a perfect fit. Pause a moment to see which ones you relate to. This can be a fun exercise to do with your spouse — as long as you don't take yourselves too seriously! (Also note that while I've given each personality type a gender-specific name, all the following types apply to both males and females.)

MONEY PERSONALITY TYPES

- *Sam the Slob:* Sam finds it very difficult to get organized, so he deals with a fair amount of clutter. Financial life is often chaotic and a source of problems, especially in marriage.
- *People-Person Paula:* Relationships mean *everything* to Paula. She finds it difficult to make managing her finances a priority. "Don't bother me with all those details," she says. She's often very generous

— sometimes to a fault. While these traits are endearing, they can lead to the same problems Sam the Slob runs into.

- *Suzy Spender:* Suzy gets tremendous short-term emotional satisfaction from buying things for herself and others. She often spends more than she has — and not necessarily on healthy priorities. She doesn't think of the consequences of this overspending until a lot of damage is done.
- *Harry the Hoarder:* Harry is like a squirrel with his money — he stashes it away, but not necessarily for appropriate needs. The hoarding is often done out of his desire to develop a sense of security. He borders on stingy by holding too tightly to what he has.
- *Wilbert the Winner:* Wilbert considers money a game. He wants to stay ahead of the Joneses and plays to win. Wilbert will often be a person of substantial accomplishment, but his drive needs to be tempered by the motive of love rather than the desire to be number one.
- *Paul the Penny-Pincher:* Paul does a great job of watching over the pennies, whether through the use of coupons or watching out for special sales. But Paul fails to look at the larger picture. He may be using coupons, but he can still be overspending. More important, he may have not taken the time to set godly priorities — for example, the education of his children.

Most of us will have *tendencies* toward a number of these types, and we should remember that not all of them are unhealthy if kept in proper balance (except maybe for Sam the Slob!). But the extremes are unhealthy. Typically, one or two of these attitudes dominate how we look at money. These attitudes are a result of who we are (including our personality), how we were raised, the impact of our friends and family, and influences from the media.

But understanding how these attitudes developed isn't really as important as learning to modify them where necessary. So now that we recognize that how we handle our money is a reflection of our interior life, how can we develop a financial "plan of life" that will guide us to true financial freedom and peace? That's the $64,000 question, isn't it?

OUR ROLE: FAITHFUL STEWARDS

No matter what personality types we relate to, God has given each of us a special calling and responsibility. We've received so much from our Lord — life, faith, freedom, and family. We've also been given talents and resources to be used in ways that are pleasing to God. He calls us to be *faithful stewards*.

Recall the scene in the Old Testament where Joshua, in his old age, reminds the Israelites of their covenant with the Lord and poses this question: "And if you be unwilling to serve the LORD, choose this day whom you will serve, whether the gods your fathers served in the region beyond the River, or the gods of the Amorites in whose land you dwell; but as for me and my house, we will serve the LORD" (Josh 24:15). Now fast-forward to the Sermon on the Mount, where our Lord provides his disciples with the foundations for living a truly Christian life. He says this:

> Do not lay up for yourselves treasures on earth, where moth and rust consume and where thieves break in and steal, but lay up for yourselves treasures in heaven, where neither moth nor rust consumes and where thieves do not break in and steal. For where your treasure is, there will your heart be also. . . . No one can serve two masters; for either he will hate the one and love the other, or he will be devoted to the one and despise the other. You cannot serve God and mammon. . . . Do not be anxious, saying, "What shall we eat?" or "What shall we drink?" or "What shall we wear?" . . . your heavenly Father knows that you need them all. But seek first his kingdom and his righteousness, and all these things shall be yours as well (Mt 6:19–33).

Scripture and Church teaching set forth two clear but divergent paths that we can take with our finances. The materialistic way of the world is characterized by love of self and love of things, while God's way is characterized by love of God and love of neighbor. The world's way leads to bondage, anxiety, and worry, while God's way leads to freedom, peace, and contentment.

How can you tell if you're following the way of the world with your finances? Recall the statistics in the introduction and consider the following questions:

- Are your life's pursuits focused primarily on the acquisition of wealth and a lot of "stuff" or on developing a deeper relationship with God?
- Is your prayer life on life-support, or is it thriving?
- Do you and your spouse argue about money matters, or is there financial peace in your home?
- Are you always scrambling to make ends meet at the end of the month, or are you living within your means?
- Do you find that your charitable giving is done after all your other bills are paid — as an afterthought — or have you learned to be generous from your first fruits?
- Do you pay your entire credit card balance off every month, or is consumer debt accumulating?
- Do you have a planned savings program where money is set aside every month for future needs, or are you spending all your current income?

Part II of this book will help you learn and apply God's principles for handling money in such a way that your relationship with him becomes more intimate and your life's purpose becomes more fulfilling.

TOOLS FOR THE JOURNEY

God has provided, through the Church, all the tools we need to help us grow in our relationship with Christ. I hope you'll seek out these gifts and apply them in your walk with the Lord. They'll bring you encouragement and hope!

The first gift is the Church itself. Christ instituted the Church and gave us Peter as his first vicar on earth to guide her. In Matthew 16:18, we read, "And I tell you, you are Peter, and on this rock I will build my Church, and the powers of death shall not prevail against it." Christ has given us assurance that we can rely on the magisterial teaching of the Church — through the pope and the bishops in union with him — to guide us on our faith journey.

The second gift is the liturgy, especially the Mass, where we worship God and where the events that saved us are not only recalled but made present in the Eucharist.[18] The whole liturgical life of the Church revolves around the Eucharistic sacrifice and the sacraments.[19] I point especially to the Eucharist and penance as powerful ways we can continue to grow in our relationship with Christ, as we are encouraged to participate in these frequently.

We've also been given God's word through sacred Scripture. Here we have the story of salvation history and God's blueprint for how to have a fulfilling life.

The *Catechism* provides a compendium of what we believe as Catholics and why. We also have an abundance of testimony and teaching from the saints — spiritual giants who have already "walked the walk." Compile a solid reading list and take advantage of these treasures.

Prayer is an essential part of your faith journey as well. It's simply "the raising of one's mind and heart to God or the requesting of good things from God."[20] Our faith offers many forms of prayer, including the liturgy, the rosary, and personal prayer. All of these bring us to a closer relationship with God. You can use them to develop an active prayer life.

Finally, what a special gift we have received in Mary, our Blessed Mother. While on the cross, Jesus spoke to Mary and his beloved disciple John when he said, "Woman, behold your son!" and (to John) "Behold, your mother" (Jn 19:26–27). As the Mother of Christ and the Mother of the Church, Mary has a special advocacy role to play for all of us with her Son. Deepen your love for Mary and ask her to help you grow closer to Jesus. That is her desire!

So how can we get our arms around these gifts and apply them in our lives so that they make a difference in our walk with the Lord? How do we keep God first amidst all of our daily responsibilities and "to-do" lists? Time and commitment are key ingredients to any successful relationship, and our relationship with the Lord is no different.

Let me draw on an analogy. When I turned 40, I realized that I needed a regular exercise routine if I was going to better maintain my health. I chose to take up cycling, and I take a 10-mile ride several days a week around the area where we live. It's rather hilly, and it works my legs and my lungs. In 1 Timothy 4:7–8, we read that physical exercise is good, but spiritual exercise is even more important. Here is what Paul said: "Train yourself in godliness; for while bodily training is of some value, godliness is of value in every way, as it holds promise for the present life and also the life to come."

Just as we need to exercise regularly to maintain our physical health, so we also need regular spiritual exercise. Here are some practical suggestions to help you apply in your daily life the spiritual gifts we've been given. I call this a daily spiritual plan, and I encourage you to make it your own.

A DAILY SPIRITUAL PLAN

Dedicate each day to our Lord upon rising with a morning offering (see Appendix A).

- Read the Bible, the *Catechism*, and the writings of the saints for 10 or 15 minutes each day.
- Attend Mass daily if possible. If not Mass, perhaps a brief visit to our Lord in the Blessed Sacrament.
- Pray the Angelus at midday (see Appendix A).
- Meditate on the life of Jesus by praying a mystery (or more!) of the rosary each day.
- Complete a five-minute review, or examination of conscience, of your day upon going to bed.
- Make a weekly holy hour (Eucharistic adoration).
- Receive the sacrament of reconciliation every two weeks.

It's through the sacramental life that we're able to deepen our relationship with the Lord, and these steps offer a time-tested path for the journey.

Here's a prayer that captures the essence of what I've been sharing. Take this prayer to heart as you begin this journey of stewardship and financial freedom.

THE STEWARD'S PRAYER

Lord,

I give you thanks for creating me and redeeming me.

Keep me close to you during all my days.

Help me to remember that life on earth is short and the life to come eternal.

Grant me a generous spirit; may I love you well by loving others well.

Guide me to a wise use of the gifts you have entrusted to me — my time, my talents, and my treasure. May I use them for your greater glory!

Divine Providence *can* provide.

Divine Providence *did* provide.

Divine Providence *will* provide.

Amen.

My hope is that you have embraced your call to be a faithful steward of the gifts God has given you. With that life-changing shift in attitude, you're ready to continue on the journey to becoming financially free!

(While it isn't the purpose of this book to provide a full discussion on the issue of holiness and how one can grow in it, I felt it was important to provide some of the basic guidelines we're given through the Church's teaching. I *highly* recommend that you read *Introduction to the Devout Life* by St. Francis de Sales for a more complete examination.)

 FREEDOM DIVIDENDS

- Make sure you and your family receive the sacrament of reconciliation at least monthly.
- Develop a solid list of faith-building reading materials.
- Implement the remainder of the daily spiritual plan as appropriate for your life circumstances.

Chapter 3

MARRIAGE AND MONEY

*M*y wife and I recently attended the wedding of the daughter of a good friends of ours. At the reception, there was a special dance for all married couples, during which the master of ceremonies began asking couples who had been married less than a certain number of years to leave the dance floor. It started with 5 years, then 10, 20, and so on. As you can imagine, after the 20-year mark, the crowd began to thin out considerably, until finally there was only one couple remaining — they had been married 47 years. Everyone spontaneously broke into applause, giving the two a standing ovation.

We all recognize the goodness of marriage. Our esteem for it is universal, and it shows when we see an example like that of the couple at the wedding. Marriage and family life are described beautifully and powerfully time and again in Scripture and in the *Catechism of the Catholic Church*. Marriage "has been raised by Christ the Lord to the dignity of a sacrament."[21] "Matrimony is intended to perfect the couple's love and to strengthen their indissoluble unity," and by grace, "they help one another to attain holiness in their married life and in welcoming and educating their children."[22] The family home is the "domestic church, a community of grace and prayer, a school of human virtues and of Christian charity."[23]

Paul's description of love in his letter to the Corinthians is classic, and many couples use it as one of the readings at their wedding ceremony. "Love is patient and kind; love is not jealous or boastful; it is not arrogant or rude. Love does not insist on its own way; it is not irritable or resentful; it does not rejoice at wrong, but rejoices in the right ... So faith, hope, love abide, these three; but the greatest of these is love" (1 Cor 13:1–13). He further describes the love between husband and wife as that between Christ and the Church — a sacrificial love (cf. Eph 5:21–33).

Then how is it that we hold marriage and family life in such high esteem and have such beautiful teachings, yet we suffer from divorce rates of around 50 percent and have so many broken homes? Why are marriages "threatened by discord, a spirit of domination, infidelity, jealousy, and conflicts that can escalate into hatred and separation"?[24] The answer rests with our fallen human nature. "According to faith the disorder we notice so painfully does not stem from the *nature* of man and woman, nor from the nature of their relations, but from *sin*."[25]

A while back I was a guest speaker at a family conference, along with a number of other presenters. I remember hearing Janet Smith, the noted author and speaker, making the point that when couples get just three things "right," the chances of their having a successful marriage and family life are enhanced exponentially. The three issues were the couple's relationship with God, their embracing of the Church's teaching on human sexuality, and managing their money using godly principles.

I agree wholeheartedly with Janet's assessment, and I believe that our society's high divorce rate can be attributed in large part to our failure in one or more of these areas. We've already seen that finances are one of the leading causes of marital breakups.

Take a moment to read the following excerpt from a letter I received expressing how money problems have led to difficulties in one couple's marriage:

> I hope you can help us. My husband and I are caught up in a terrible financial struggle, and the tension is killing our marriage. We're very committed, but the joy has gone out of our everyday lives. My husband has two jobs, but between the mortgage, life insurance, energy bills, car insurance, taxes, and so forth, we haven't enough to make ends meet. We've cut all expenses to the bone, but we still don't have enough for food or gifts or emergencies, and now we're in a lot of debt. . . .

It has always been a curiosity to me that the vast majority of time I get requests for advice, the call comes from a woman. It must be a "guy" thing that keeps men from asking for guidance. Yet here's a letter from a man in the Midwest who poured his heart out regarding his financial difficulties. I guarantee that many men are feeling what he has conveyed:

> My wife and I have been married for twenty years, and our finances have been in shambles from the very start. Why? I don't really know. Maybe ignorance, or maybe just trying to have immediate gratification. As the world tells you, "You can have it all."
>
> It all came to a head in the last two years when I lost my $70,000-per-year job as sales manager at forty years of age. With five beautiful children ranging in ages 2 to 17, it came as quite a shock. For a little over a year, I worked two, three, and sometimes four jobs to bring in money to pay bills. But with my salary cut almost in half, our debt load escalated from $8,000 to over $20,000 — and it's not been good for any of us. In fact, it's embarrassing.
>
> To believe two college-educated persons could mess up so bad is hard to face and imagine. If you can guide me, I would very much appreciate your help. It's such a blessing to see someone in the Catholic Church addressing the issues of financial instability. It's long overdue!

DEVELOPING A SENSE OF UNITY

How can a couple establish a solid foundation in their marriage when it comes to their finances and avoid the strains on the relationship shared by the two couples who wrote me the preceding letters? By learning to do a few basics well, you'll find that your finances will be an area of strength in your relationship rather than a source of stress and conflict.

The first — and I believe the most important — step you can take as a couple is to develop a sense of unity in terms of how you look at money. God calls husbands and wives to be one: "Therefore a man leaves his father and his mother and cleaves to his wife, and they become one flesh" (Gen 2:24); "what therefore God has joined together, let not man put asunder" (Mk 10:9). Now is the time for you to commit to a life of stewardship as a *couple*, committing yourselves to managing your money according to the godly principles found in sacred Scripture and Church teaching.

Couples often enter marriage with very different perspectives on money. One spouse may have been raised in a home where money was plentiful, while the other might come from a background where every penny had to be watched. How do two unique individuals create the type of unity I'm referring to? By looking to Christ and his example, the two begin to move closer together as they strive to imitate his perfect love — and fully live out their sacrament of marriage.

MEN AND WOMEN: REAL DIFFERENCES

It's important for husbands and wives to recognize that there will be some pretty profound differences between them. The late Larry Burkett once said that if two people who were the same got married, one of them would be unnecessary!

One of the bigger differences between men and women tends to be in the "why" we choose to do something. In general, women tend to be more "heart"-oriented. Their emphasis is on the relationship. Men, on the other hand, tend to be focused on the end result — that is, the goal.

I remember hearing author and speaker Gary Smalley sharing an experience he had with his wife. He thought it would be a nice thing for him to take her shopping for the day. He knew she liked to shop — even though he didn't. He figured it would be a good way for them to have some quality time together.

His wife made one minor mistake as they got to the mall: She mentioned that she needed a blouse. While Gary had been all set to spend a leisurely day with his wife and was happy just to be with her, he was now on a mission.

As they entered the first store, they began looking at blouses. To Gary, any number of them seemed just fine, but not to his wife. They left the first store empty-handed, and Gary could feel his frustration growing. This scenario repeated itself several times until they finally left the mall without the coveted blouse! Gary's irritation reached a peak before he finally realized that he had turned what should have been a very relaxing time with his wife into a hunting adventure!

This same type of experience can occur between spouses when it comes to managing their money. The husband may jump into the budgeting exercise immediately, holing up for a day to input their income and expenses into the latest, greatest software package. When finished, he proudly shows his wife their new budget — and lets her know where she needs to make spending adjustments. He can't understand why she doesn't seem to appreciate his efforts!

It's interesting to see how men and women look at spending and investing decisions. It's not unusual for a husband to think his wife spends too much money on things like clothing and gifts for others (unless of course, the gift is for him — then it's okay!). And it may be true — she may be overspending in these areas. But I often find that men are blind to the fact that they have some very expensive hobbies as well. It may be golfing or ballgames, and yet they don't recognize the impact these items have on their family's finances.

I've noticed a similar trend when it comes to investing. Women tend to want an investment plan that recognizes their desire for security, while men have a tendency to want a plan that achieves the greatest return possible — even if that means taking a higher level of risk. Consider the example of a man who wants to invest in a business by using the equity in their house. While many men would feel comfortable doing this, many wives would feel very *uncomfortable*. You see, to the woman it's not just a house; it's her family's home, and putting it at risk creates a sense of unease. The decision to borrow against the equity in the home doesn't recognize that security is important to her.

When it comes to spending and investing decisions, it's important for spouses to openly discuss and agree on major decisions. By doing so, you'll avoid making some big mistakes, and you'll maintain the sense of unity that's so important for the health of the marriage.

A TEAM EFFORT

Another area of difference between husbands and wives will be the talents they bring to the marriage. Both spouses need to be involved in the overall financial picture, but it works best for one of them to handle the basics — including bill paying, checkbook management, and keeping the budget updated.

Normally within a marriage, one or the other spouse has a stronger gift when it comes to handling details. In 1 Corinthians 12:4–7, we read how God has dispersed gifts differently: "Now there are varieties of gifts, but the same Spirit; and there are varieties of service, but the same Lord; and there are varieties of working, but it is the same God who inspires them all in every one. To each is given the manifestation of the Spirit for the common good." The spouse who has the greater eye for detail should be the one who handles these responsibilities.

But one person's natural inclination to handle the financial details doesn't let the other off the hook! A critical part of maintaining the sense of financial unity in the marriage is in coming together periodically to review the status of the budget. I like to call these "family budget meetings," and you should have these *at least* every quarter. If you're just starting out, you'll want to have them more frequently — I'd suggest at least monthly.

The idea behind these meetings is for the spouse handling the financial details to have prepared a summary level budget with updated actual income and expenses. It's a good idea to provide the other spouse with a copy ahead of the meeting, so they have time to see where things stand.

The meetings are a great opportunity to review the goals you've established and see if things are going according to plan. Are the "bigger picture" items working out the way you had hoped? Is your budget balanced? Are you giving and saving at appropriate levels? Maybe you'll find that spending in a particular area is running higher than what you'd planned, and you need to brainstorm on how you can bring it back in line. Maybe there's been a life-changing event, such as the birth of a new baby, that'll require changes to the budget. In the meeting, you can look forward and anticipate issues that will affect you down the road.

I can't overemphasize the fruits that come from cooperation and teamwork. I find that whenever there is a major issue confronting our family, a much better decision gets made if my wife and I discuss the pros and cons first. She brings out points that I fail to consider, and vice versa. Proverbs 15:22 tells us that our Lord designed it that way: "Without counsel plans go wrong, but with many advisers they succeed."

Here is one final note on teamwork and budgets: It's really important that the budget be used as a tool and *not* as a weapon. Too often a spouse will use it to get what he or she wants or as a way of putting the other spouse down by minimizing the things that are important to him or her. It's crucial to always listen to your spouse and respect the ideas he or she brings to the discussion.

MAKING IT ON ONE INCOME

Raising children isn't easy with the negative trends toward a materialistic and (we might as well admit it) rather hedonistic society. It has become more important than ever to provide a wholesome environment for kids to grow up in, and that often means having Mom or Dad stay home full time and surviving financially on one income.

First of all, it *is* possible for many families to make it on one income today, even though society tells us differently. Certainly you'll need to manage your money with great care and skill. Proper budgeting and a simplifying of your material expectations will be key components of a successful plan.

You may also be surprised to hear that in many situations a second income may actually be *costing* your family money! It's easy to think of our gross income as the amount being added to the family coffers, when in reality we incur a great number of expenses just to hold a job. When all these costs are considered, you may find that you're working for less than minimum wage, or even losing money.

Here's what I mean: Let's assume you're planning on working 20 hours per week, and you anticipate an hourly rate of $15 per hour. Your *gross income* would equal $15,600 per year. But because two-income families find themselves extra tired and squeezed for time, they'll typically spend a great deal more on convenience items, resulting in substantially higher costs. The following simple income statement provides an example of how a second income may be spent:

Gross Income		$15,600
Less:		
Tithe	$1,560	
Taxes (estimated at 30%)	4,680	
Higher food costs	2,000	
Auto costs	3,000	
Child care	3,500	
Clothing	1,000	
Meals out	1,000	
Total expenses		$16,740
Net loss		$ 1,140

These amounts are estimates and may differ from your own situation, but you should go through the same exercise with your own figures. You might be surprised when you see the results. Here's what one woman had to say after the budgeting exercise showed she *could* stay at home:

> My husband and I have been married just over a year and were excited about starting a family right away. Neither of us had a large amount of savings, and both of us had school and credit-card debts, so I was convinced that I'd have to work at least part time after the baby to make things work. My husband was convinced otherwise. He used your worksheets and proved to me that I could be a full-time homemaker.
>
> Our daughter is two months old now, and I couldn't be happier! It isn't easy, especially living in the ultra-expensive Washington, D.C., area, but it's so worth it. We're encouraging all our friends to go through this same process right away.

After completing your own analysis, maybe you'll find, like the woman who wrote this letter, that you can fulfill your dream of staying home for your family.

There are really countless ways you can make ends meet on one income. Here are some specific suggestions that will help stretch your resources:

- Make sure you have an annual budget, which will be your financial road map. Remember, when we fail to plan, we're planning to fail. I remember reading somewhere that, unfortunately, 95 percent of Americans don't budget, which is part of the reason so many find themselves in financial trouble.

- Avoid consumer debt. Interest charges on credit cards and other forms of consumer credit take vital funds away from your family. If you use credit cards, pay them off *every month*. If you're already in debt, use the Accelerator Repayment Plan in Chapter 8 to get out of debt now!

- Housing is typically the most substantial item in a family's budget. Too frequently I see couples overextend themselves on their "dream home," causing a great deal of anxiety and pressure because there isn't enough money left to meet their other needs. When making a housing decision, don't wait for the bank to tell you how much they'll loan you. Instead, develop a realistic budget, take it to the bank, and show them what you can afford. Also, keep an eye on interest rates. Depending on the circumstances, refinancing your home can be a simple way to save money.

- Transportation costs are substantial for most families. Are two cars truly a necessity? Are automobiles a hobby for you that take up an inordinate amount of time and money? If you financed or leased your car, the interest is costing much more than you think. Save up so you can pay cash next time.

- How many tasks do you pay to have done that, with a little effort and know-how, you could do yourself? Changing oil in the cars, winterizing the home, using cloth diapers, cutting children's hair, mowing the lawn, sewing clothes, and learning how to do simple repairs all offer great opportunities for the family to stretch its budget.

- Do you find yourselves eating out frequently? Even an inexpensive outing every few weeks may be too much for many families.

- When grocery shopping, do you purchase cereal, cookies, soda, chips, frozen dinners, and other prepared foods? While there are times when this may be necessary, it's a very expensive option.

Purchasing staples in bulk, baking your own bread, canning, and gardening all offer healthy and inexpensive ways to feed the family.

- When it comes to entertainment and recreation, much that our society offers is not only expensive but not very wholesome for the family. The key to family recreation is making time for one another, not spending a lot of money. Taking walks or riding bikes, playing ball in the yard, and picnicking are all free and offer great family fun.

Here's one final thought: In a one-income home where Dad is the provider, it's possible to underestimate the additional burdens placed on Mom as spending on "convenience items" is cut back. My wife has a friend who raised a large family in the 1950s and 1960s. Money was always tight, and she often found herself crying at the kitchen sink while doing the dishes from the overwhelming stress of managing all that had to be done. Most moms I know are stretching themselves to the limit for their families. Husbands need to be there with an encouraging word *and* a helping hand.

STRAIGHTFORWARD ADVICE FOR ENGAGED COUPLES

How can young couples prepare themselves so they can avoid the money problems that afflict so many marriages? There are a number of steps that should be taken, and parents, friends, and pastors can play a key role in preparing engaged couples so they'll enjoy lifelong and fulfilling marriages. Here are a few suggestions:

- Get your spiritual life in order. You'll be amazed at how this directly impacts your finances.
- Determine who will handle the basic financial duties and focus on making finances an area of good communication.
- Create a financial plan (budget) for the first year of your marriage.
- Learn how to manage your checkbook.
- Discuss the use — and misuse — of credit.

One of the common mistakes I see young couples making is spending well beyond their means when planning their wedding and setting up their first home. Unfortunately, I see too many of these couples put tens of thousands of dollars on credit cards in order to have a large wedding and fancy reception. Then they open charge accounts at department stores and purchase several thousand more dollars in furnishings. Add to this the fact that many engaged couples also have substantial student loans to pay back. While the wedding and honeymoon are like a dream come true, managing the debt afterward can be a living nightmare.

Assuming that newlyweds start out with two incomes, I advise them to live on one and save the entire second income. Not only will they learn the discipline of saving (it's much easier to save *before* children arrive), but they'll also find that it allows for the option of having a parent stay home full time when blessed with offspring. If both incomes are spent from the start, the couple may find it extremely difficult to change their lifestyle to reflect the reduced income.

One of the best gifts an engaged couple can give themselves is to create a financial plan (budget) for the first year of their married life *before* the wedding. I recommend that they locate a mentor couple who can review their proposed budget and offer suggestions. In the event they can't find another couple, they could ask their parents, pastor, or a friend to fulfill this role. This will set the stage for effective planning and communication on money matters throughout their marriage.

A budget should be a reflection of your priorities, and your priorities should be formed by your faith. That's why it's so important for spouses to study what our Lord has to say about money before jumping into the actual plan. By studying Scripture and Church teaching together, praying, and discussing how the principles you learn apply to your particular situation, you can create a strategy that honors God and your family.

 FREEDOM DIVIDENDS

- Determine who will take responsibility for handling the financial basics.
- Set a regular schedule for your family budget meetings.

Chapter 4

CHILDREN
AND MONEY

THE EARLY YEARS

*C*hildren have a built-in curiosity that allows them to soak things up like a sponge. It's a wise parent who understands this and goes about building the character of the child in the virtues early on. The *Catechism of the Catholic Church* reminds us that "The *role of parents in education* is of such importance that it is almost impossible to provide an adequate substitute" (*GE* 3) (CCC 2221). In teaching your children about money matters, you'll want to emphasize the development of a Christian attitude in addition to showing them the practical skills they'll need to properly manage their money when they leave home.

There's probably no greater influence on the attitude of your children than your example. Are you satisfied that your priorities are following the gospel message? Is God first in your life? Are you fostering the virtues of simplicity, generosity, sacrifice, and personal responsibility in your home? Your living model is a more valuable blessing to your children than any material inheritance you may provide. Pope St. Gregory the Great once said, "For true doctrine tries both to teach by words and example . . . when one practices first and preaches afterwards, one is really teaching with power."

One approach you can use to teach your children about financial responsibility is to reward them monetarily for completing tasks around the home. A good time to start is when your child reaches the age of reason (about seven for most kids). This is a simple and effective way to introduce them to the concept of pay for work, and it avoids an "allowance" where the child is receiving something for nothing. Remember, a good workman is worthy of his wage. When our second daughter was six years old (a saver if there ever was one), she proved to be quite industrious at collecting snails in the yard to earn money. In fact, each spring she had quite a bonanza!

When you begin paying your son or daughter for chores, set up a system that divides the earnings into three categories: set aside 10 percent for their tithe; another 10 percent for long-term savings; and then allow your child to spend the remaining money, or put it into short-term savings in order to build up enough cash to make a more substantial purchase, such as a bicycle.

THE TEEN YEARS

As your children enter the teen years, you should have three goals for their financial education. First is to continue the work of helping them develop a faith-filled attitude toward money. Second is to teach them how to use the basic tools of financial planning. (A great way to accomplish both of these is to work through the material in this book with them over a period of months.) Your third goal is to give them the opportunity to apply their understanding by permitting them greater control over the portion of the family budget that directly impacts them.

Let me give you an example. A good category to start with is clothing. Determine the teen's budget for the year, and hand over the responsibility for managing it. You might be surprised at the lessons learned as a result of this exercise. I've heard parents share stories of their teens blowing the money at back-to-school time on a few expensive name-brand items. When these wear out during the course of the following months, or other clothing needs arise, the teen begins to realize that money doesn't grow on trees! It can be a good thing for them to feel some of this pain while under your roof, so they learn to make better decisions once they're on their own. Continue adding to their area of responsibility as you deem appropriate, always keeping in mind that tithing and saving need to be factored in to the income you're providing.

56

Before your teens leave home, make sure you have taught them the importance of managing money from a faith-filled perspective, as well as the following basics of money management:

- Together, walk through the 7 Steps to Becoming Financially Free in Chapter 7.
- Make sure your children have their own checkbooks during their later teen years. Make sure they're responsible for managing it, including reconciling the monthly bank statement.
- Warn your teens of the danger of credit card debt and other forms of consumer credit. Help them realize that credit and debit cards aren't inherently problematic, but that their misuse can create financial havoc. Stress the importance of paying credit card bills off in full every month.
- Show them how to develop an annual budget. Have them prepare a budget for their first year away from home before they leave, and review their plans with them. Remember, by this time they should be establishing their own priorities. Your job is to provide your insights and answer questions when asked.
- Show them how saving early brings incredible benefits through compound interest (see example in Chapter 11).
- Walk them through the basics of investing. They should know what mutual funds are and how to monitor the performance of the assets that they've invested. They should also understand the benefits of saving tax-free or tax-deferred money through qualified retirement plans once they begin working.

THE PRODIGAL CHILD

What if you have a rebellious adult child who is acting irresponsibly with money? With grown children, bad habits may make the job more difficult, but just as with the prodigal son, our Lord continually calls us back "home." Look for an opportunity where your son or daughter would be open to suggestions. I've frequently found that many young couples (engaged or newly married without children) may not be ready to hear about such things as budgeting and prioritizing expenses. They're often still starry-eyed — thinking they'll be in a financial position to satisfy all their whims.

Yet when that same couple has their first child, it's amazing to see the changes that take place. All of a sudden, the new parents seem to grasp the magnitude of the job ahead of them and realize — maybe for the first time — that resources will be limited. This can be an opportune moment for you to reach out to them. Share what it was like for you and your spouse to manage the affairs of your family, including the more difficult times. Let them know that God has a design for life that leads us to true freedom — even in the area of our finances.

If your children are in the midst of a true emergency, but appear ready to become more responsible, you may want to offer assistance to "buy" the time needed so they can assess where they are and develop a plan for the future. The process of getting on a budget may take a month or two. You may choose to help them with such things as utility and grocery bills during this time. To what extent you offer further help will require prudent judgment. On the one hand, if your children have learned their lesson, have developed an effective plan, and are following through on it, I see nothing wrong with providing additional assistance. This can be a good way to reinforce responsible behavior and help them learn good habits that will last a lifetime. (Your assistance should probably be a gift rather than a loan, since lending money to family members can have serious implications on your relationship.)

On the other hand, if your children show no signs of changing their ways, you can expect them to continually come back to you for help. In this case, it may be better for them in the long term if you apply a little "tough love" and hold out until they're willing to demonstrate change.

MEDIA AND CHILDREN

The media have become a major force to be reckoned with in the lives of children today. The television is on for more than 8 hours a day in the average American household.[26] Kids between the ages of 6 and 11 are watching about 23 hours of TV per week.[27] In addition, many children between the ages of 6 and 14 have access to various media in their own bedroom: 69 percent have television; 35 percent have cable or satellite; and 18 percent have Internet access.[28]

The successful rearing of children depends on a number of things, but two of the most important include the love, involvement, and example of both parents; and the development of the child's character in the virtues. The Bible gives parents the following admonition: "Train up a child in the way he should go, and when he is old he will not depart from it" (Proverbs 22:6). When parents allow their children to spend such large amounts of unchecked time in front of the TV and computer, they're abdicating their responsibility to form their children to the media and advertising industries.

How does the pervasive reach of media impact our children when it comes to money? First is the obvious issue of advertising, much of which is targeted at children, with the expectation that these kids will apply pressure on their parents to buy what they want. Examples of this abound at Christmastime, when a particular toy becomes the fad for the year. Parents stand in line for hours and spend ridiculous amounts of money for something, purely as a result of a desire placed within their children — thanks to the constant bombardment of advertising. This in turn makes it difficult to develop the virtue of temperance.

The second effect may be even more sinister. While there was a day when most television programming was fairly benign, with the likes of *I Love Lucy* and *The Andy Griffith Show,* much has changed since then. The levels of graphic violence and sexuality have increased substantially, especially with the addition of cable and satellite. This makes the task of teaching our children about a virtuous life much more difficult than it used to be. Imparting a Christian sensibility to your children regarding money can't be done in a vacuum. You can't effectively teach your children about a godly attitude toward money, then have that message undermined by programming and advertising that has content that so often is contrary to the values we hold dear.

Don't let the TV and Internet be destructive influences for your kids. There is certainly some programming worth watching, but even then the time should be limited. We have found that when we leave the TV off, the kids get outside and find creative and wholesome ways to have fun. We have also had a tradition of making Friday nights our family movie nights. We have a library of good DVDs and videos that we can enjoy together.

CATHOLIC HIGHER EDUCATION: A TWOFOLD PURPOSE

I find it interesting, maybe providential, that as I put together my thoughts on higher education, I'm at a Catholic college with my oldest daughter and son and a number of their friends. We're making a three-day visit to the school as we begin to discern this next stage of our children's education. With my oldest going off to college soon, and six other children behind her, we've spent a great deal of time thinking through the purpose of higher education as well as how to fund it. I'd like to share my thoughts on both topics here. I see two primary purposes when it comes to higher education, especially as it relates to young Catholics. These include their ongoing development as a whole person in the image of Christ; and the development of their vocational skills, whether their calling is to the priesthood or religious life, family life or the single state.

The early college years, where young people are typically between 18 and 22 years old, continue to be a time of searching about who they are and how they fit into this great big world. This is a time for them to consider the more important questions about life, to solidify what they believe and why, and to do so in an environment that will foster a closer relationship with the Lord. A solid Catholic liberal arts education helps young adults find answers to these important life questions. It also helps young people place their vocation in the context of this bigger picture.

When it comes to young adults' particular career callings, it's important to remember that the dizzying pace of change in technology that has led to a global marketplace requires that our children be well-equipped to play their part in that economy. For many, that will mean obtaining an education beyond a core "Catholic liberal arts" formation — that is, one that's focused on particular vocational training, such as medicine, law, business, nursing, teaching, and so on. I'm a strong advocate of coupling a solid Catholic liberal arts program of study with the best vocational education the young adult can obtain.

Another point that shouldn't be overlooked is that the college years frequently lead to the choice of a spouse as well as obtaining a degree. Because of this, I can't overstate the importance of selecting a school that places your children in an environment that draws students who love and practice their Catholic faith.

It's also important to remember that a college education may not be the right choice for each of your children. Not everyone is of the "bent" to complete a four-year (or longer) academic program. Much time and money can be wasted trying to force a square peg into a round hole! We all have different gifts and abilities, and some of us would do better to learn a trade or craft through an apprenticeship or vocational trade school.

PAYING FOR COLLEGE

Making financial plans for the higher education of children is a daunting task for any parent. Some choose to avoid the issue while their kids are young, assuming they'll be able to deal with it later. Unfortunately, this is the last thing you want to do. One of the most important steps you can take toward being able to provide your children with a solidly Catholic college education is to start saving for it early. This helps you take advantage of compound interest — getting your money to work for you!

The College Board (www.collegeboard.com) estimates that one year of college education today, including room and board at a public four-year university, totals $12,127, while a private institution totals $29,026! Assuming 4-percent inflation and an after-tax investment return of 10 percent using a tax-qualified savings plan, you would need to save $416 per month from the day your child is born in order to fully fund the cost of a private school. Before you pull your hair out, remember that very few people actually pay the full listed price. Still, this can be an important wake-up call to get on a budget and plan your savings ahead of time. Also, remember that in addition to your own savings, there are a number of other things you can do.

Over the last few years, the federal government has enacted various legislation designed to ease the financial burden of higher education, including the Hope Scholarship Credit, Lifetime Learning Credit, Educational

IRAs, and 529 Savings Plans (additional information is provided on these topics in Chapter 12). And don't forget the possibility of scholarships and grants. Depending on your child's scholastic abilities and extracurricular activities, as well as your financial situation, these may provide a substantial portion of the overall college cost. The College Board's website, www.collegeboard.com, can be a very helpful tool for better understanding how you can pay for your son's or daughter's college education.

You shouldn't feel that you need to finance the complete cost of your offspring's education. Children may have a greater appreciation for their education if they pay for a portion of it. Participating in school work programs and using money from summer jobs can be a healthy way of achieving this. You'll want to ensure that work doesn't become an end in itself. Otherwise, your children's grades may suffer, with negative consequences for the future.

One strategy I recommend highly is paying off your mortgage by the time your oldest child reaches college age. By doing so, you can free up a sizeable chunk of resources that can be applied to college expenses. While that doesn't eliminate the need to save specifically for college, it certainly eases the bite when the time comes.

One final issue — and one that I feel strongly about — is student loans. As you know, I'm a believer in minimizing one's debt. It can make sense to use debt prudently *when you're purchasing an appreciating asset.* Most often, this relates to the purchase of a home and possibly investment real estate, but it also holds true for obtaining a higher education. Many studies have shown that a college degree adds significantly to one's earning potential over the years. So taking on some debt to obtain a college degree can make sense if done prudently. But doing so also comes with risks.

I remember visiting with a young man who had gone into about $70,000 worth of debt to finance a law degree. Once he completed his schooling, he realized he really didn't want to practice law, so he didn't end up with the income he thought he would. People need to be realistic about the level of debt they take on in relation to their major. Going into debt for a significant amount of money when you expect to choose a profession with a relatively low salary means that you'll have the burden of the debt around your neck for a long time.

Finally, remember that many young people marry shortly after finishing college. College loans become an especially heavy burden when coupled with the need for a home and the starting of a family. With planning, creativity, and sacrifice, you'll be in a position to help your children receive a solid college education without breaking the bank or getting buried far too deep in debt. The *7 Steps to Becoming Financially Free Workbook* provides further information on how you can develop a plan to assist the funding of your child's college years.

PASSING ON A REASONABLE INHERITANCE

You've seen motor homes traveling down the road with a bumper sticker on the back that says, "We're spending our kids inheritance." I get a chuckle out of that one. For many, inheritance issues necessarily take a backseat to just trying to meet their family's current needs. I hear many Catholic families say that a child's college education is their inheritance!

Still, there are a couple thoughts I'd like to pass on with respect to providing your children with an inheritance. Many people spend all they have and leave a legacy of debt, while others pass on levels of wealth that their children aren't prepared to deal with. Scripture reminds us to keep a balanced perspective. Proverbs 13:22 says, "A good man leaves an inheritance to his children's children." Yet, Proverbs 20:21 says, "An inheritance gotten hastily in the beginning will in the end not be blessed."

So what would a balanced perspective look like? I think it starts with the concern mentioned in Proverbs 20:21. I've seen too many examples of young people losing their perspective on life because they inherited large sums of money. So, if you'll have a reasonable level of wealth to be passed on, make sure you factor in the ability of your children to manage it with a godly perspective. You might be better off leaving them with a lesser amount that assists them with their housing and education needs, as well as funds to develop a business, but gives the excess away for other good causes. You certainly won't want to give them so much that they could just sit around and do nothing with their lives. Be sure to keep in mind the long-term needs of any disabled children, for whom ongoing assistance will be required. Trusts can be used to ensure that they're taken care of appropriately when you're no longer around.

 FREEDOM DIVIDENDS

- Develop a "work-for" allowance system for your younger children. Guide them toward giving away 10 percent and saving 10 percent before spending the remainder.
- Hand over increased budget responsibilities to your teens for things like clothes and entertainment. The time for them to learn to develop priorities is now, before they leave home.
- Use the *7 Steps to Becoming Financially Free Workbook* to develop a plan to pay for your children's college education.

Chapter 5

WORK: A PATH TO HOLINESS

*W*hile work is not the primary topic of this book, it obviously plays a substantial part in our personal finances, and there are some important principles to talk about. Not long ago, I was asked by a friend to speak to a group of business leaders about "Faith in the Workplace." I started the discussion with a quote from the apostolic exhortation *Christifideles Laici,* "On the Vocation and the Mission of the Lay Faithful in the Church and in the World," promulgated by Pope John Paul II. Number 59 in that document says, "There cannot be two parallel lives in their existence; on the one hand, the so-called 'spiritual' life, with its values and demands; and on the other, the so-called 'secular' life, that is life in a family, at work, in social relationships, in the responsibilities of public life and in culture." That is a powerful statement. The Pope reminds us that we can't separate our faith from our work. Our faith isn't for Sundays only, but is meant to be lived out every day of the week.

Dr. Arthur Stehly, a Catholic obstetrician and gynecologist who delivered most of our seven children, has been a great example of living out his faith in the workplace. During the 1980s, he had no qualms about prescribing contraceptives to his patients. When he heard Pope John Paul II speak during a visit to Southern California, Dr. Stehly was convinced he needed to bring his medical practices in line with the teaching of the Church.

He went to confession and mentioned his dilemma to the priest, saying that he felt called to phase out his dispensing of contraceptives. The priest — it seems to me with the hand of Providence guiding him — asked Dr. Stehly if he were a bank robber, would he "phase out" his robbing of banks, or would he stop immediately? Dr. Stehly realized he needed to stop dispensing contraceptives without delay.

Returning to his office, he wrote a letter to all of his patients, letting them know of his decision. What was the immediate reward for this act of faithfulness? Two-thirds of his patients left his practice! I'm sure you can imagine the financial impact of removing two-thirds of your revenue base from your business. Yet within two years, he found himself busier than ever. What happened? When pro-life families heard about this doctor — one that appreciated their openness to life rather than one who would try to convince them to practice artificial contraception or be sterilized — they began flocking to him. Before long, his practice was booming. He had the courage it took to trust in God's providence, and he was rewarded. He has been a great inspiration to us, and an example of integrating faith and work.

FAITH AND WORK

How does your faith intersect with your work? While the answer will depend in part on the type of work you do and the role you play, our faith calls all of us to fulfill certain responsibilities. Here are some starter questions for you to consider:

For Employees

Many families I counsel find themselves in financial bondage largely because they haven't developed a strong work ethic. Poor work habits can result in an inability to attain a higher paying job and even unemployment. A proper attitude toward work is a key not only for financial success, but also for spiritual growth. The *Catechism of the Catholic Church* says, "*Human work* proceeds directly from persons created in the image of God and called to prolong the work of creation by subduing the earth, both with and for one another (Cf. Gen 1:28; *GS* 34; *CA* 31). Hence work is a duty: 'If any one will not work, let him not eat' (2 Thess 3:10; cf. 1 Thess 4:11). Work honors the Creator's gifts and the talents received from him. It can also be redemptive" (CCC 2427).

As an employee, are you taking the following steps so that you'll be a valued employee? By doing so, you'll assure a more stable financial future for your family.

- Do you exhibit the highest levels of integrity to your employer? Dishonesty often starts with "small" things. Do you steal time or supplies from your employer? Do you fudge on your expense account? Trust is critical in the employer/employee relationship.
- Are you a diligent employee? Employers appreciate workers who "Plan the work and work the plan." Follow through on the commitments you make and do your work right the first time.
- Are you a positive influence in the workplace? Be helpful to your co-workers. Be on guard against jealousy or envy with co-workers.
- Ask your supervisor how you can improve and how you can be of greater value to the organization.
- Seek to improve your skill levels through continuing education.

For Employers and Managers

What do you see as the purpose of your business? Is your *primary* motive to seek a profit, or is it to bring greater glory to God? How do you view your competition? Are they enemies you seek to eliminate, or do they help you be of greater service by making you better at what you do? Have you considered ways you can work together for a greater common good (maybe special works of charity)?

How do you deal with your employees, vendors, and customers? Do you offer a living wage, reasonable benefits, and good working conditions? While most businesses today have caught "customer satisfaction fever" as a way of increasing market share, do you treat *everyone* you deal with fairly, in accord with their dignity as human beings? Are you honest in your dealings or does the pursuit of profits cause you to shortchange your obligations to people? Are you a good steward when it comes to taking care of the environment, so that future generations will be able to enjoy the resources God has provided?

Is tithing only for individuals, or for businesses, too? I just read of a start-up business on the East Coast that tithes on its pre-tax profits. The owner explained that the culture of giving is the glue that holds her company together. Not a bad example!

How effectively are you balancing your own work and family life? As the owner or key executive in the business, are you setting policies that allow your employees to have a proper balance? Remember, work is for man, not man for work.

How effectively do you witness your faith in the workplace? Do your co-workers look up to your example? Are you consistent, fair, and considerate of the needs of others? Do you take appropriate opportunities to share your faith with the people around you? Some companies find creative ways to include faith-related materials as part of their products. A favorite burger chain in California has John 3:16 printed on their drink cups. A regional airline hands out a favorite Psalm when passing out snacks. What could you do to spread the gospel?

WORK AND OUR RELATIONSHIP WITH GOD

Our society places such a great emphasis on work — often to the extent that we think we *are* what we *do*. Yet, by falling into the trap of workaholism, where we put all of ourselves into our job and have nothing left for our Lord or our families, we create a real imbalance in our lives. We tend to search for fulfillment through success and growth in our work, as well as the material benefits we receive, and yet we know that none of these will provide lasting fulfillment.

Mel Gibson, director of *The Passion of the Christ*, once said that he found himself "on the summit of a secular utopia," yet he wasn't happy. He had everything that the world had to offer, including fame and money, but there was no contentment. Only when he placed the Lord first in his life did he find the happiness he was looking for, and out of that came his blockbuster film on the Passion. Psalm 127:1–2 reminds us, "Unless the LORD builds the house, those who build it labor in vain. Unless the LORD watches over the city, the watchman stays awake in vain. It is in vain that you rise up early and go late to rest, eating the bread of anxious toil, for he gives to his beloved sleep." This doesn't minimize the commitment our work calls us to, but it does recognize that we need to keep it in balance.

In Chapter 2, "Faith-Driven Goals: Our Response," I laid out a daily spiritual plan. The plan may seem daunting at first, given a busy work schedule. Yet, what I have found over the last many years is that as one begins to incorporate it into one's daily life, the desire to spend more time with the Lord grows, and the time is made available. Just as I have found that we can make the 90 percent go further than the 100 percent when it comes to tithing money, so it is with our time. By setting our priorities more effectively, we find time to spend with our Lord and fulfill the work and family responsibilities he has given us.

WORK AND FAMILY RELATIONSHIPS

Workaholism impacts our families negatively, just as it does our relationship with the Lord. In Genesis 2:24, we read, "Therefore a man leaves his father and his mother and cleaves to his wife, and they become one flesh." Are you and your spouse living that verse out in its fullness — not just physically, but mentally and emotionally as well? Do you communicate with your spouse regarding the important issues going on at work? Do you value his or her counsel as a trusted adviser? I know that for Chelsey and me, an important part of each evening is touching base when I get home. The children know that Mom and Dad take a few moments to talk about the events of the day. We also take extended walks together a few times each week. These provide a great way for us to share with each other the successes and difficulties we're encountering. I appreciate the insight that Chelsey brings to many of these situations. She'll often have a more objective way of looking at the situation than I could ever have — and her objectivity usually brings about ways of resolving issues that I never considered.

Providing for the physical needs of our children is certainly one of the reasons we work. But our kids' needs go well beyond the basics of food, shelter, and clothing (and even mobile phones and I-pods!). Just as spending time with the Lord and with our spouse is a key part of growing those relationships, so it is with our children. This is true not only during the early formative years, but especially so during the teen and young adult years. We live in a society that forces our hand on this — with so many cultural influences that draw our children away from the values we hold dear.

We need to be involved with their formation on a consistent basis, guiding them to a firm and lasting relationship with Christ. This can only be done by spending time with them.

There is a famous song entitled "Cat's in the Cradle," written by Harry Sandy and Chapin, which captures the essence of what I'm talking about. Here are the lyrics:

My child arrived just the other day.
He came to the world in the usual way,
But there were planes to catch and bills to pay.
He learned to walk while I was away.
And he was talking 'fore I knew it, and as he grew,
He'd say, "I'm gonna be like you, Dad,
You know I'm gonna be like you."

Chorus:
And the cat's in the cradle and the silver spoon,
Little Boy Blue and the Man in the Moon.
"When you comin' home, Dad?"
"I don't know when, but we'll get together then.
You know we'll have a good time then."

My son turned ten just the other day.
He said, "Thanks for the ball, Dad, come on let's play.
Can you teach me to throw?"
I said, "Not today. I got a lot to do."
He said, "That's okay."
And he walked away, but his smile never dimmed,
And said, "I'm gonna be like him, yeah.
You know I'm gonna be like him."

Chorus

Well he came home from college just the other day,
So much like a man I just had to say,
"Son I'm proud of you, can you sit for a while?"

70

He shook his head, and he said with a smile,
"What I'd really like, Dad, is to borrow the car keys.
See you later. Can I have them please?"

Chorus

I've long since retired, and my son's moved away.
I called him up just the other day.
I said, "I'd like to see you if you don't mind."
He said, "I'd love to, Dad, if I could find the time.
You see my new job's a hassle and the kids have the flu,
But it's sure nice talking to you, Dad,
It's been sure nice talking to you."
And as I hung up the phone, it occurred to me,
He'd grown up just like me.
My boy was just like me.

Chorus

You've heard it said before that we are only passing through in this life, and whether it's our possessions or our work, we can't take them with us. We have such a short time to be with our children during their formative years (even though sometimes it seems as though the day will never end!). Our ability to help them grow in their relationship with Christ, their brothers and sisters, and their fellow man passes ever so quickly. I encourage you to maintain an effective balance between your faith, family, and work. Keep in mind what efforts offer the greatest dividends, and place the majority of your time, talent, and treasures toward those goals. The love of family is a gift that will span eternity.

LEARNING TO DELEGATE

One of the more common causes of workaholism is having the belief that no one else can do our job as well as we can. This attitude stems from a lack of humility. As a result, we fail to develop others and delegate to them in a responsible way. It's especially important for leaders to focus on getting the big picture right, to take time to attract, train, and empower good people to help them reach their goals.

Consider the story of Moses in Exodus 18:13–27. Moses is acting as an intermediary between the Lord and the Israelites. He finds himself working from early morning until late in the evening making judgments on the disputes that the people are bringing to him. His father-in-law sees what is happening and says, "What is this that you are doing for the people? Why do you sit alone, and all the people stand about you from morning till evening? . . . What you are doing is not good. You and the people with you will wear yourselves out, for the thing is too heavy for you; you are not able to perform it alone."

Moses' father-in-law goes on to teach Moses how to find capable people who can resolve the lesser issues while bringing those to him that truly require his attention. Now rather than spending all of his time trying to plug a leaking dam with his finger by adjudicating every case, Moses focuses on finding men capable of handling tens, hundreds, and thousands, freeing him up for the duties that he was called to.

So if you find yourself in the trap of workaholism, and you can see that at least part of the reason is a lack of prudent delegation, I encourage you to learn how to hand on responsibility to others. Done properly, it will provide growth opportunities for you, your staff, and your organization. This also applies in the home. Many stay-at-home parents take on all of the chores because they want them done "their way," instead of teaching their children to take a more active role in the family.

WORK AND COMPETITION

Competition is a double-edged sword. We're used to competition in sports, scholastics, and business, and we seem to thrive on it. Competition certainly has a way of pushing us to enhance and refine our skills, and this is a good thing. But when the competitive spirit leads to an attitude of domination, it becomes a spiritual problem. If we are honest with ourselves, we'll recognize that we often measure ourselves against others in order to satisfy our own egos, and provide a sense of our superiority.

This is the reverse of what we find in Scripture. We read the following in Philippians 2:3–8:

> Do nothing from selfishness or conceit, but in humility count others better than yourselves. Let each of you look not only to his own interests, but also to the interests of others. Have this mind among yourselves, which was in Christ Jesus, who, though he was in the form of God, did not count equality with God a thing to be grasped, but emptied himself, taking the form of a servant, being born in the likeness of men. And being found in human form he humbled himself and became obedient unto death, even death on a cross.

As Catholics, we would say the Pope fills the most important office in the world. Yet, one of his titles is "Servant of the Servants of God" — meaning the servant of his fellow bishops and priests. So we see this paradox of great authority combined with great humility. That's the model we should be emulating.

In the classic Christmas movie *Miracle on 34th Street,* Gimbel's and Macy's are heated competitors. Kris Kringle plays the department-store Santa for Macy's. When children ask for something the store doesn't have, rather than try to talk them into another present, he tells the parents to go to Gimbel's. At first, his boss reprimands him — after all, Macy's wants to make the sale. But after a while, Macy's realizes that the practice ends up being so good for business that it encourages it throughout the store. Gimbel's starts doing it as well. True, it's only a movie, but it does reflect a better view of how we should treat customers and competitors. We need to develop a deeper humility!

The life and teaching of St. Thérèse of Lisieux can be a great example to us. She lived and taught that our smallest acts, done with love, are a great offering to God. We are called to *transform* our motive for acting from a desire to "win" to a desire to "love and serve." This perfected motivation inspires us to develop our talents and use our skills even more effectively than when we act out of selfishness.

ADDITIONAL RESOURCES

If you own a business or take part in running one, I encourage you to read the following materials that will help you further grow in your understanding of the relationship between your faith and work. First are two papal encyclicals, *Rerum Novarum* (On the Working Class) and *Centessimus Annus* (On the 100th Anniversary). *Rerum Novarum* was written in the late 1800s by Pope Leo XIII. He saw the threat of communism coming and wrote, among other things, about the right to hold private property. *Centessimus Annus* was written by Pope John Paul II on the 100th anniversary of *Rerum Novarum*. It was written shortly after the fall of the Berlin Wall and of communism in Russia. The Pope wrote about the weaknesses of communism, but also challenged capitalist-based systems to keep the dignity of man at the forefront, rather than profit. They are like bookends when it comes to a discussion of economic issues, and I highly recommend them. They are available at the Vatican's website, www.vatican.va.

Remember the guiding principle from *Christifideles Laici* that I opened with: "There cannot be two parallel lives in their (lay faithful's) existence; on the one hand, the so-called 'spiritual' life, with its values and demands; and on the other, the so-called 'secular' life, that is life in a family, at work, in social relationships, in the responsibilities of public life and in culture." I encourage you to begin on this path of transforming your life of faith, work, and family.

 FREEDOM DIVIDENDS

- Whether you are an employer or an employee, do you act with utmost integrity at work?
- Sit down with your spouse and talk about how well you are balancing work with the other responsibilities in your life, including your relationships with the Lord, your spouse, and your children.

Chapter 6

GIVING AND GROWING

*Y*ou remember the story of Ebenezer Scrooge in the delightful Charles Dickens novel *A Christmas Carol.* Although fictional, he has become the epitome of what it means to be uncharitable — shown most often by his poor treatment of his clerk, Bob Cratchit. There are real-life Scrooges we can point to as well, including Howard Hughes, J. Paul Getty, and Cornelius Vanderbilt. These men built or inherited empires, and even though they had immense wealth, they either spent it lavishly on themselves (as in the case of Hughes) or they hoarded it. A different example is St. Katharine Drexel. Katharine also inherited a great deal of wealth, but she dedicated it to the improvement of Native Americans and African Americans in the late 1800s and early 1900s. Katharine was canonized on October 1, 2000. It would be easy to oversimplify the differences between America's actual Scrooges and St. Katharine Drexel, but it's fair to say that the lives of Hughes, Getty, and Vanderbilt were a sad tale of selfishness, while St. Katharine Drexel's was one of genuine charity.

The subject of giving comes up frequently in Scripture, yet it remains one of the most misunderstood concepts in Christian living today. On the one hand, we see many television preachers promoting a "health and wealth" gospel — sort of a "give-to-get" mentality, which most people recognize as a false gospel. On the other hand, many stewardship sermons focus solely on funding new buildings, school programs, or missionary activities — messages concerning a physical need. When we limit our understanding of giving to providing for the material necessities of the Church — worthy though they may be — we've missed its primary purpose.

75

WHY DO WE GIVE?

We give for a very simple reason. That's what God tells us to do in the Bible. It's a good assumption that God doesn't need the money, so why has he made giving such an important part of his revealed word? He knows that it's easy for us to turn inward when it comes to how we handle our money. *The call to give is itself a gift from God that helps us grow in our love for him and our fellow man.* The prophet Malachi wrote to an Israelite people whose love for God had grown cold. The animals they offered in sacrifice were blind and lame, rather than the choicest of the herd, and they weren't being faithful with their tithe:

> From the days of your fathers you have turned aside from my statutes, and have not kept them. *Return to me, and I will return to you,* says the LORD of hosts. But you say, "How shall we return?" Will man rob God? Yet you are robbing me. But you say, "How are we robbing thee?" In your tithes and offerings! You are cursed with a curse, for you are robbing me; the whole nation of you. Bring the whole tithe into the storehouse, that there may be food in my house; and thereby put me to the test, says the LORD of hosts, if I will not open the windows of heaven for you and pour down for you an overflowing blessing (Mal 3:7–10, emphasis added).

God calls the Israelites back to him by telling them to be faithful in their giving, but giving is also about our relationships with our fellow man. When Jesus spoke of the final judgment, he referred to a separating of the sheep and goats. He places the sheep at his right hand and invites them to inherit the kingdom:

> "For I was hungry and you gave me food, I was thirsty and you gave me drink, I was a stranger and you welcomed me, I was naked and you clothed me, I was sick and you visited me, I was in prison and you came to me." Then the righteous will answer him, "Lord, when did we see thee hungry and feed thee, or thirsty and give thee drink? And when did we see thee a stranger and welcome

thee, or naked and clothe thee? And when did we see thee sick or in prison and visit thee?" And the King will answer them, *"Truly, I say to you, as you did it to one of the least of these my brethren, you did it to me"* (Mt 25:35–40, emphasis added).

When we give, we give to Christ himself. The previous passage reminds me of the life of Mother Teresa of Calcutta and her work on behalf of the poorest of the poor. She consistently said she saw Christ in those she served.

I remember hearing noted apologist Scott Hahn speak about giving. With his typical play on words, he spoke of the "tithes that bind." That short phrase captures the essence of what giving is all about: God doesn't want us to give because he needs our money; he wants us to give so that our hearts can grow. When we give, we remember that all we have comes from God and that we're completely dependent on Him. We grow in humility, trust, and gratitude, and our love of God and neighbor grows more consistent and we overcome our fickle nature. We give because we love (see 1 Cor 13:3).

HOW DO WE GIVE?

Giving takes various forms in Scripture, including the tithe and various offerings. It's clear in numerous places in the Old Testament (Lev 27:30-32, for example) that the tithe was the model provided by God for supporting divine worship and meeting the needs of the poor.

Tithing is also mentioned in the New Testament, where an interesting transition begins to take place. In Matthew 23:23, our Lord chastises the Pharisees for being *legalistic* about how they tithe, not for tithing itself. He wants a conversion of heart, but lets them know they should continue in good works: "Woe to you, scribes and Pharisees, hypocrites! For you tithe mint and dill and cummin, and have neglected the weightier matters of the law, justice and mercy and faith; these you ought to have done, without neglecting the others."

The generous spirit the Lord is looking for is further conveyed in 2 Cor 9:6-7: "The point is this: he who sows sparingly will also reap sparingly, and he who sows bountifully will also reap bountifully. Each one must do as he has made up his mind, not reluctantly or under compulsion, for God loves a cheerful giver."

St. Irenaeus takes this thought a step further: "Thus the people of Israel used to dedicate tithes of their possessions. But those who have been given freedom devote what they possess to the Lord's use. They give it all to him, not simply what is of lesser value, cheerfully and freely because they hope for greater things, like the widow who put into God's treasury her whole livelihood." You can see in these verses the transition from a legalistic approach to giving into the concept of stewardship. All we have is the Lord's and he has entrusted us to manage it in ways pleasing to him.

In Canon 222 of the *Code of Canon Law,* we read that "The Christian faithful are obliged to assist with the needs of the Church so that the Church has what is necessary for divine worship, for apostolic works and works of charity and for the decent sustenance of ministers. They are also obliged to . . . assist the poor from their own resources." You'll notice that this is an *obligation,* but Canon Law doesn't define how we are to *practically fulfill* the obligation.

In the *Summa Theologiae,* St. Thomas Aquinas provides a detailed discussion of tithing (II–II: 87). He concludes that the tithe is not for the Old Testament people only, but arises partly from natural law and partly from the institution of the Church. He also concludes that the Church, based on the requirements of the time, can ordain the payment of some different amount (II–II: 87:1).

Today the Church does not require that we give 10 percent of our increase. But it does require that we support both it (the Church) and the poor, and the practice of tithing has strong precedence in the Bible and Church history. Catholics currently give about 1 percent of their income for charitable purposes — well below the 10 percent tithing model provided in Scripture.

Can we truly say that we're giving our best to God, or are we acting more like the Israelites during the time of Malachi? I believe that we've been overly influenced by our materialistic culture and that we tend to give as an afterthought, rather than from our first fruits. As a result, we're missing out on many of the Lord's blessings. Remember the words of Malachi where God tells us to "put me to the test." I encourage you to make tithing a part of your spiritual and financial life and see what blessings the Lord has in store for you.

TITHING PRINCIPLES

All we have comes from God. He owns it all (see Dt 10:14). Through tithing, we learn to place our trust in God's providence. He has promised to provide for all our needs (see Mt 6:30–34). Almsgiving is provided by God as one form of penance, along with prayer and fasting (see Tob 12:8–10; CCC 1434). Additionally, God can multiply our resources and make 90 percent go further than 100 percent — remember the accounts of the widows and the miracle of the multiplication of the loaves and fish (1 Kings 17:7–16; 2 Kings 4:1–7; Mt 14:13–21)?

We are called to be cheerful givers (Acts 20:35; 2 Cor 9:6–7), and our giving should be voluntary (Mt 6:2–4; 2 Cor 8:1–5). A typical response from people who tithe is that they enjoy paying their tithing "bills" as opposed to their regular bills.

HOW TO BEGIN

Giving should be planned, not done haphazardly (see 1 Cor 16:1–2). Pay your tithe as your first bill to follow the principle of giving from your "first fruits" (Prov 3:9–10). In the usual situation, I suggest you give half your tithe to your parish and the remainder to other worthy purposes. Then review your amount periodically and adjust for changes in income. Ask yourself the following question: *Would God be satisfied with my charitable works if he saw my checkbook?*

Deciding that you *want* to tithe will be a key to being able to do so. The tithing journey is one that requires both stepping out in faith and personal responsibility. While some families decide to increase giving immediately to a full tithe, in most cases I encourage them to take an incremental approach — especially when there are other financial problems. If a family is currently spending 110 percent of its income and starts tithing without making any adjustments, they'll find themselves spending 120 percent of their income and falling deeper into debt. While we need to trust in our

Lord's providence as our heavenly Father, we also need to know that he expects us to use the tools at our disposal to properly manage our finances. Here are some suggestions:

1. Complete an overall review of your finances to get a better understanding of where you stand.
2. Your next step will be to create an initial budget, which factors in an increase in your giving from, let's say 1 percent to 3 percent, and includes appropriate amounts for debt repayment. Does your new budget balance? If not, you'll need to come up with cost-saving ideas to implement until it does.
3. Once your initial budget is completed, you'll want to track your income and expenses to verify that your actual results are in line with your budget. You'll find the budgeting tools you need in the *7 Steps to Becoming Financially Free Workbook*.

Once you've completed the steps noted above, I'd encourage you to "test" our Lord (see Mal 3:7–10) by increasing your giving by a percentage or so every few months. At the same time, "work" your budget to keep it balanced. Keep your desire to tithe in prayer, and while it may take a couple years to reach a full tithe, you'll find that keeping God first in your finances has positive ramifications on many other areas of your life as well.

Here's a table that can help you determine the tithe based on various income levels:

TITHING GUIDELINES			
Annual Income	Annual Giving at 1%[29]	Annual Giving at 10% (Tithe)[30]	Monthly Tithe
30,000	300	3,000	250
40,000	400	4,000	333
50,000	500	5,000	417
75,000	750	7,500	625
90,000	900	9,000	750
105,000	1,050	10,500	875

TRUSTING IN GOD'S PROVIDENCE

A key to being a good steward is to achieve a balance between *trusting* in God's providence as our Father and being *prudent* in our planning. Here's a story that can help us learn better how to apply these principles.

St. Maximilian Kolbe, a Franciscan priest, is best known for his heroic death in the Auschwitz concentration camp and his deep devotion to Mary. One of the works that Kolbe is less known for is a family magazine he published. When he first came up with the idea for the periodical, he sought the approval of his superior. Recognizing the good that the project would do, the superior gave his okay, but let Maximilian know that the order could not help him financially. Having planned the project, Maximilian knew that he'd already raised half of the funds necessary and he felt confident in starting this new venture.

But just halfway through the project, Maximilian ran out of money and was bitterly disappointed that he'd failed in this important endeavor. In prayer before the Blessed Sacrament, he expressed his disappointment and feelings of failure. As he got up to leave, he noticed an envelope on the altar, marked "For You, Immaculata." Inside was just enough money to complete the project.

Closer to home, I remember when I was involved with the launch of the daily radio program *Catholic Answers Live*. Through planning and prayer, we concluded that a daily live call-in program could do much good in teaching and explaining the faith. The time came when we had to commit to building the studio — at a cost of $20,000. The bill would be due upon receipt of the materials (in about 10 days) and we didn't have that money set aside. With our staff and families praying, we moved ahead with the purchase, and within three days, received a check from a woman in the Midwest for $20,000. I remember one of the staff saying, "I guess we were supposed to get involved in radio!" We were all awestruck by God's choosing to provide for us in this way.

On the other hand, I also remember undertaking projects where adequate funding didn't materialize. After prayer and our best efforts, we had to recognize that these projects must not have been the path God wanted us to follow.

A key point here is that trusting in God's providence doesn't mean that we fail to plan or go against the principles of finances he has provided in Scripture and Church teaching. While we were stretching ourselves financially to undertake the radio program, we had a solid plan in place and we didn't take any risks that might endanger the apostolate.

Achieving balance in this area is a challenge. It comes most effectively when we're rooted in prayer and truly place ourselves at God's disposal to do as he desires. Whether you're dealing with financial issues related to your family, business, or apostolate, learning to balance prudence and trusting in God's providence is a key to being a good steward.

FREQUENTLY ASKED QUESTIONS

Tithing on Net or Gross Income

People often ask whether the tithe should be based on gross income or net income. Today, it's your choice as to whether you want to base your tithe on your income before taxes (gross income) or your income after taxes (net income). However, tithing on gross income (before taxes) is the biblical precedent. In the *Summa Theologia,* St. Thomas Aquinas notes that, "Tithes are due on the fruits of the earth, in so far as these fruits are the gift of God. Wherefore tithes do not come under a tax, nor are they subject to workmen's wages. Hence it is not right to deduct one's taxes and the wages paid to workmen before paying tithes: but tithes must be paid before anything else on one's entire produce" (II:87).

Tithing on Low Income

Aquinas briefly addresses the issue of the needy paying tithes and concludes that they should, but also notes that the Church has a responsibility to assist using the tithes received. You can see how if we were faithfully living this out the Church and poor would *both* have sufficient resources to meet their needs.

Remember the account of the moneyless widow who was heroically generous by using the last of her flour and oil to prepare a little cake for Elijah (1 Kings 17:7–16). After her generous act, the Lord provided enough flour and oil so that she and her son were able to eat for a year.

The words of Pope Leo XIII in *Rerum Novarum, On the Condition of the Working Classes,* should provide comfort when he says that, "No one, certainly, is obliged to assist others out of what is required for his own necessary use or for that of his family." So if your resources are very limited, I encourage you to be as generous as you can, but don't make imprudent decisions when it comes to your basic needs and those of your family.

Tithing and Catholic School Tuition

Is it appropriate for families to have a portion of their tithe apply to Catholic school tuition? The Church teaches that parents are the primary educators of their children, and providing them with a proper formation certainly falls within the activities described in section 222 of Canon Law (noted earlier). Your decision will depend on your willingness to objectively review your financial situation and apply the virtue of temperance in your financial life. It would be common in our materialistic society for families with sufficient wealth to tithe and pay for their children's education to feel they didn't have the resources to do both.

Whatever your income, I encourage you to take the following steps as you strive to make a decision that pleases our heavenly Father. Take another look at your budget and your overall financial position. Even if a family believes that it would be impossible to reduce spending, a fresh and objective look at the situation would be a good place to start. Once you've analyzed your income and expenses and reviewed your budget, place this issue in prayer before the Blessed Sacrament and ask our Lord's help in making a decision that honors Him.

Also, don't forget to be creative when looking at the cost of educating your children. If your children attend parochial schools, take this opportunity to discuss your situation with the school and investigate the financial-assistance programs that are offered. Some Catholic schools offer substantial discounts for larger families. Contact the school and research the different possibilities. Have you considered home-schooling? It can be much less expensive than most private schools, especially in the early years.

If you find that the only way you can afford a Catholic education is by using virtually your entire tithe, I would recommend that a minimal amount (for example $5 per week) be committed to your parish via a weekly donation. Our Lord can multiply the amount and at the same time, the visible nature of the gift will provide a good example for your children.

Tithing on Investment Gains

Generally speaking, our charitable giving should be based on our increase. Certainly interest, dividend, and capital-gains income are part of our increase, so how should we go about tithing on our investment income? Here are a few items to consider.

On the one hand, there are always current needs within both the Church and society at large that we should keep in mind. There is merit in giving today to help feed someone who is hungry, or meet some other temporal need. There is also a great need to re-evangelize much of the world, and providing resources today so that this new evangelization can be accomplished is also good. So with these thoughts in mind, it would certainly be a positive thing to make a current contribution out of the increase in your investments.

On the other hand, if the account is a retirement account and there would be penalties associated with a distribution, it's definitely reasonable to wait until your retirement years (when the distributions are made) in order to make your gift.

Giving Guidelines for the Wealthy

The founder of one of the companies I worked for is very blessed financially. He's also a strong believer in tithing and has been very generous to the community over the years. He understands that there is a special responsibility that comes with increased wealth, and has often said that the hardest job he has is in determining whom he should give to. If you've been blessed financially, you'll have important decisions to make about the lifestyle you set for yourself and the amount of giving God is calling you to. In many cases, sacrificial giving would call for generosity in excess of the tithe.

Whom to Give to

When considering whom we should be giving to, Scripture and Canon Law provide helpful guidance. Scripture shows a preference for the poor (Prov 21:13; Gal 2:9–10) and teachers of the faith (1 Tim 5:17–18; Gal

6:6). Canon Law emphasizes the need to give for divine worship, the decent sustenance of priests, the support of apostolic works, and to help the poor (Section 222).

CONCLUSION

Some people fall into the trap of a scrupulous attitude toward tithing, but a greater number are lax in their willingness to increase their charitable giving. Neither of these extremes is what our Lord calls us to. American Catholics give about 1 percent of their income for charitable purposes. Most families need encouragement to reach for the 10 percent figure because they've been overly influenced by society's acquisitive attitude. Pope John Paul II often spoke about how we've become a society of *having* rather than *being,* and tithing is one certain way to rearrange our priorities and turn our hearts back to God. It's an important tool for overcoming the materialistic drive so prevalent in our world.

I've seen case after case of individuals seeking happiness through the pursuit of material goods — only to realize that these never lead to fulfillment. Instead, the pressure of maintaining a lifestyle beyond one's means (especially if it is built on a mountain of credit) often leads to a breakup of the family and even the loss of faith.

People who tithe, on the other hand, find that the worries and anxieties they once had are replaced by contentment as they learn to place love of God and neighbor above their desire for things. They also find that they become much better stewards of the resources God has given them. When families with financial problems — such as habitual overspending, high debt levels, and a lack of savings — apply God's principles for handling money, they begin to bring order to what has been a chaotic situation.

I remember hearing from a Virginia woman about the impact tithing had on her family. She'd been trying to get her husband to tithe for years, without success. After reading one of my articles on the subject, he decided to give tithing a try. She went on to share the transformation that occurred in their family over the next few months as his heart was turned back to God, to her, and to their children. *That's what tithing is all about!*

FREEDOM DIVIDENDS

- Have a family discussion about your giving. Commit to a life of generosity. Discuss whom you feel called to give to, and remember to keep in mind God's preference for the poor.
- Work with your children during their early years to establish a generous spirit through tithing — the lesson will stick with them for life.

Part II

ACHIEVING FINANCIAL FREEDOM

Chapter 7

7 STEPS TO BECOMING FINANCIALLY FREE

*A*rchbishop Fulton Sheen, one of the great teachers of the faith during the 1950s and 1960s, was in Philadelphia walking from his hotel to the convention center to give a seminar. On the way, he got lost. He came upon some boys playing basketball. "Where are you going?" they asked. "To give a talk on how to get to heaven, but I'm lost and need help finding the convention center. Would you care to join me?" he said. They shot back, "Not really. If you can't find your way to the convention center, what makes you think you know the way to heaven?" Children have a funny way of getting right to the point, don't they?

Just as Archbishop Sheen got lost on his way to the convention center, people often get lost in the maze of their personal finances. In earlier chapters, I emphasized the importance of keeping the big picture in mind as it relates to your spiritual life. The same holds true when it comes to managing your money.

Most people recognize that they need a plan for their finances, but they get overwhelmed with the details of budgets, taxes, repaying their debts, and starting a savings and investment strategy. I'm sure many would rather get a root canal than have to develop a financial plan! They feel intimidated and, as a result, give up before they've even started.

It's not necessary for a financial plan to be complex. True, there may be times when certain details get complicated — that's when you need to ask for help from a competent professional. But your overall financial plan should be straightforward and understandable.

It's important that your financial plan be driven by your life plan. It should support your desire for a strong walk with the Lord, a committed marriage and family life, the formation and education of your children, and

89

7 STEPS TO BECOMING FINANCIALLY FREE

 STEP ONE Be a "Steward of Providence"

 STEP TWO Assess Where You Are – Develop a Plan

 STEP THREE $2,000 Emergency Savings

 STEP FOUR Eliminate Debt – Accelerate It!

 STEP FIVE Rainy-Day Fund – Six Months' Expenses

 STEP SIX Review Insurance and Estate Planning Needs

 STEP SEVEN Save and Invest with a Purpose

meeting the needs of your retirement years. Your life's goals should drive your plan, not the other way around. As you read about the various steps to becoming financially free, take a moment to consider where you're at. If you find yourself just starting out, don't get discouraged! What's important is that you understand where you are and where you want to go.

While the specifics of a financial plan will vary with each person's circumstances, most plans will have much in common. After all, so many of our lives follow similar paths. We get out of school and start our career, purchase our first car, get married, and establish our first home. Then we have children and go about raising them as best we can, and before we know it, they're leaving home for college and we're entering the retirement years.

I call these the "big picture" stages of life, and they relate to important steps on your journey to financial freedom. While I'll cover these steps in greater detail in later chapters, let's review them briefly here.

STEP ONE: BE A "STEWARD OF PROVIDENCE" (MATTHEW 25:14-30)

As we've already discussed, the most important financial decision you'll make is committing to being a faithful steward of the gifts God has entrusted to you. It starts with getting your spiritual house in order, recognizing that all you have ultimately belongs to God, learning to be generous with the tithe as your model, applying temperance to your lifestyle, and developing effective communication in your marriage.

STEP TWO: ASSESS WHERE YOU ARE — DEVELOP A PLAN (LUKE 14:28-30)

I remember reading somewhere that about five percent of Americans live on a budget. It shouldn't be a surprise that so many are getting into "wrecks" on their financial journeys. Unless you prioritize how your money will be spent, you'll find that it will grow legs and run away. Learning how to put together a budget and committing to living on one is Step Two. (I'll provide more information on creating and keeping on a budget later in this chapter.)

STEP THREE: $2,000 EMERGENCY SAVINGS (PROVERBS 21:20)

In this stage, you'll set aside $2,000 into an emergency savings fund. You might be thinking, *Hang on just a minute! I've got credit card bills that are charging double-digit interest rates. Why not pay those down rather than save $2,000?* The reason I want you to set up an emergency fund is to help you break the cycle of spending that created your credit card debts in the first place.

Credit-card problems typically occur because of two issues. The first is when you habitually spend beyond your means. You'll fix this problem by developing and living by a spending plan using the *7 Steps to Becoming Financially Free Workbook*. The other big reason for this type of debt is because some kind of emergency or "surprise" occurs. It may be an urgent car repair or an emergency-room bill for one of the kids. Whatever it is, without this $2,000 savings buffer, the only option seems to be paying by credit card.

By the way, most of these surprises aren't really surprises anyway. They're just things that don't happen on a regular schedule — and we are grateful they don't! But we can and should plan for them. You can expect your cars to need repairs periodically, and the washing machine wasn't built to last forever. A good budget will make allowances for expenses such as these. By setting aside $2,000 into this emergency fund, you'll avoid adding to your credit card balance the next time one of these irregular events occurs.

 ## STEP FOUR: ELIMINATE DEBT — ACCELERATE IT! (PROVERBS 22:7)

This is a critical step on your journey. Until you eliminate your credit-card debt, you won't be able to make progress with your plan, because too many resources will be swallowed up paying high interest charges. I'll cover the details of how you can eliminate your credit-card debt once and for all in the next chapter, but suffice it to say that it will be a giant step on your way to financial freedom.

STEP FIVE: RAINY-DAY FUND — SIX MONTHS' EXPENSES (PROVERBS 21:5)

Once you've set up your $2,000 emergency savings fund and paid off your credit cards, it's time to set aside additional reserves for a rainy day. We live in a highly mobile society with an economy that's constantly shifting based on changes in technology, the country's demographics, and consumer desires. It's not like it was a few generations ago where you could expect to go to work for a large company, stay there for 40 years, and retire with your pension.

I recently spoke to a woman whose husband had been laid off twice in the last year. They had no savings and funded the shortfall with credit cards to the tune of $10,000. I want you to avoid this scenario. Setting aside six months' worth of living expenses recognizes that there may be periods of transition or even illness that you'll be confronted with. Let's work to get ahead of the curve by setting up a reserve fund for such a situation. Hopefully you'll never have to tap into it, but if you do, it's a whole lot better than going into debt with your credit cards.

 ## STEP SIX: REVIEW INSURANCE AND ESTATE PLANNING NEEDS (1 TIMOTHY 5:8)

While most of the steps to becoming financially free follow in sequence (with a bit of crossover), this step becomes especially important once children enter the picture. There may be times when it makes sense to have appropriate insurance coverage and estate plans in place before children arrive, but it's *imperative* that husbands and wives make appropriate plans once they are blessed with children. Insurance can be a confusing topic, and I'll cover the basics in Chapter 10.

When it comes to estate planning, it really makes sense that, at a minimum, you have a will. Otherwise you're leaving all decisions about guardianship of your children and the disposition of your assets up to the court. For most people today, having a trust set up in addition to their will also makes sense. It has become quite affordable to have an attorney create a trust, and the benefits are numerous — including avoiding the cost and time delay of probate, which you will incur even with a will.

In addition to providing instructions for the disposition of your assets, it's important for your estate plans to provide for the guardianship of your children in the unlikely event that both parents die unexpectedly. This decision requires a great deal of discernment. So often, we assume that one of our family members should have responsibility for guardianship. But what do you do in the event that none of them are practicing the faith? You may want to consider whether close friends who share your religious commitment and have the same core values might be better equipped to raise your children in a godly manner.

Finally, given the state of our health-care system, it has also become important to have appropriate health-care directives as part of your planning — directives that honor the Church's teaching upholding life. The National Catholic Bioethics Center (www.ncbcenter.org) has published a wonderful little guide that can help you incorporate an appropriate health-care directive into your estate plans. It's called *A Catholic Guide to End-of-Life Decisions,* and I encourage you to obtain a copy.

While it's possible to create your estate plans inexpensively using prepackaged kits, I believe you'll be better served by having a competent attorney review your particular situation and create your plans for you. It's well worth the investment.

 ## STEP SEVEN: SAVE AND INVEST WITH A PURPOSE (GENESIS 41)

Wow — just think of it. By the time you have reached Step six, your credit card debts are eliminated and you have six months' living expenses set aside. Now with the money you were using to accomplish these goals, you can start funding major purchases with cash on hand rather than financing them. This might include a down payment on a home, if you don't yet own one. It should also make it easy for you to save cash for future automobiles and other big-ticket items. What a great feeling to know that the next car you purchase is fully paid for the day you drive it away!

Your budget should now have room to start a more aggressive savings plan so that you'll have the resources you need to pay down the mortgage on your home faster, help with the cost of your children's education, and provide for your retirement years. Given the state of Social Security, you'll want to take responsibility for the bulk of your retirement needs. While each plan will be unique based on personal circumstances, in general I recommend setting aside 10 to 15 percent of your gross income for these purposes. I'll discuss saving and investing in greater detail in Chapters 11 and 12.

So there you have it. You've just been given the steps to follow to reach true financial freedom. Wouldn't it be nice if you were just a passenger along for the ride and your chauffeur took care of getting you safely to your destination? I'm sorry to tell you this, but there are no free rides! It just so happens that *you* are the driver, and to get to where you want to be, you'll have to take the steering wheel. Remember that this is a lifetime journey and your progress will be uneven. But by following the path of stewardship, you'll find the peace and contentment that God wants for you.

IT ALL STARTS WITH A PLAN

In *David Copperfield,* Charles Dickens wrote, "Annual income twenty pounds, annual expenditure nineteen six, result happiness. Annual income twenty pounds, annual expenditure twenty pounds ought and six, result misery." Isn't that so true?

To succeed on your journey, it's absolutely necessary for you to develop a spending plan for the resources God has entrusted to you. Have you noticed that money seems to have legs attached to it? If you don't tell your money where to go, you'll find it disappears quickly and you'll wonder where it all went. Instead of you managing your money, it'll be managing you!

Your plan should honor God and your family by prioritizing spending in a manner consistent with godly principles. This system is often called a *budget* or *cash flow plan.* It's the tool that provides direction for your spending and gives you momentum to reach your desired destination.

As a Christmas gift, our pastor recently sent all the families in our parish a wonderful book called *The Christian Home,* written by Fr. Celestine Strub, O.F.M., in 1934. The author talks about the importance of families keeping a budget in the following way:

The best way for parents to avoid excessive or ill-advised expenditures is to keep a family budget. Let them make a careful study of their resources and a classified list of their needs; e.g., housing, food, clothing, running expenses, improvement, and savings. Then let them fix a certain percentage of their income for each of these items of expense, and hold their disbursements strictly within the budget allowance, unless real necessity or charity require otherwise. Keeping a home and a family is just as much a business as running a store; so why should it not be kept on a business basis? Many couples have had their eyes opened by keeping an itemized account of disbursements. They found that they had been extravagant without realizing it. But if keeping tab on one's expenses teaches economy, it should be done in every Christian home; for economy, supernaturalized, is nothing but the Christian virtue of moderation.

If keeping a home was just as much a business as running a store in 1934, it's certainly more so now, with such things as variable-rate mortgages, complex insurance and investment options, automatic teller machines, credit cards, and a tax system that's nearly impossible to understand.

Too often, people assume that a budget is a one-time event. They sit down, summarize their past spending, and put down what they think is reasonable for the future. While this is a good start, it's only the beginning. A well-run business doesn't just set a budget and stop there. It tracks what actually occurs, compares those results to what was projected, and makes appropriate adjustments along the way. The same should be true for how you manage your personal finances.

It'll take a few months to develop a budget that's realistic. I often chuckle when reviewing the initial plan of someone I'm counseling. They may be deep in credit card debt, but the budget often shows a surplus. In reality, they've underestimated certain types of spending and have often left out entire expense categories.

I remember counseling one couple who had estimated $30 per month for meals out. I asked how often they ate out, what type of restaurant they went to, and whether they took the kids (they had a large family). They admitted that they took the whole family out for pizza once a week and that it cost about $30. The annual budget they had prepared allowed for $360, while they were actually spending closer to $1,500. Imagine that type of error multiplied across five or six spending categories. Pretty soon you're talking about real money!

Don't be surprised if it takes about three months to determine whether your budget is a good reflection of your actual spending. To provide you with a bit of a head start, I've developed a "guideline budget" for different income levels and assigned spending percentages for each of the main categories.

GUIDELINE BUDGET — PERCENTAGES						
Gross Income	30,000	45,000	60,000	75,000	90,000	105,000
Tithe/Giving	10%	10%	10%	10%	10%	10%
Taxes	4%	12%	13%	15%	18%	20%
Current Education	-	-	1%	1%	2%	2%
Savings and Investments	5%	5%	7%	9%	9%	10%
Housing	38%	35%	33%	31%	30%	28%
Groceries	13%	12%	11%	11%	9%	9%
Transportation	13%	12%	11%	10%	9%	8%
Medical/Dental	4%	3%	3%	3%	3%	3%
Insurance	4%	3%	3%	3%	3%	3%
Debt Payments	-	-	-	-	-	-
Clothing	3%	2%	2%	2%	2%	2%
Entertainment and Recreation	3%	3%	3%	3%	3%	3%
Work Related	-	-	-	-	-	-
Miscellaneous	3%	3%	3%	2%	2%	2%
Total Spending Percentage	100%	100%	100%	100%	100%	100%

This guideline budget is only meant to help you get started. After you've successfully tracked your expenses for a few months, you'll be in a position to develop your own budget, which will take into account your special circumstances and priorities. It's not important that your spending agree with the guideline in every area, but it *is* critical that your expenses not exceed your income. It's also crucial that your spending plan reflect godly principles. Therefore, giving, education, and savings are all high priorities, and you need to plan for them just like any other expense.

FINAL NOTES ON THE VALUE OF A BUDGET

Let me touch on a few more items that are key when it comes to budgets. There are basically three general options you have as far as budgeting systems go. You'll find all of the information you need in the *7 Steps to Becoming Financially Free Workbook* to help you understand which option is best for you, as well as instructions on how to get started. But I'll give a brief description here.

Your first option is to use a computer-based budgeting system, of which several are available, including the subscription-based "My Budget" section at www.VeritasFinancialMinistries.com. This provides information similar to what the forms in the *7 Steps to Becoming Financially Free Workbook* do, but makes the process more efficient, since much of it is automated. You might also consider Intuit Quicken, or Microsoft Money. The second option is to develop your budget and track your expenses by hand using the forms in the *7 Steps to Becoming Financially Free Workbook*. The forms provide all you need to understand where you are with respect to your assets and debts, as well as your income and expenses. This way, you'll have records of your spending readily available for your review at any time.

Finally, the third option is to use a basic envelope system where you have an envelope for each category of spending. Your monthly budgeted amount for each category is noted on the envelope, and you divide the cash from your paycheck according to those figures. You use the money you've set aside in each envelope during the month, and when the money is gone, you don't spend again until the next month. This is the simplest method and can work very well if you haven't been able to stick with one of the other two options, which are more complete but also more involved.

Remember that a budget is a tool that should enhance communication in your family. It shouldn't be a mechanism to control your spouse. When used properly, it brings husband and wife together and helps them establish proper spending priorities. It helps them look ahead and anticipate issues that they need to deal with. As a result, families are able to respond to potential problems before they turn into a crisis. When used in this manner, a budget truly sets you free.

You can expect a few bumps along the way, especially during the early stages of developing and learning to stick with a spending plan. I remember hearing from good friends of ours after they'd created a budget. They had a large number of children, and as they looked for ways to reduce expenses and make the budget balance, the children would moan and groan about some of the cutbacks. I was affectionately nicknamed "the hatchet man"! Be aware that there may need to be some painful changes to habitual spending habits, but don't get discouraged. It takes a few months to get used to how budgets work and to begin seeing the benefits. Remember the words of St. Josemaría Escrivá, "To begin is for everyone, to persevere is for saints."

 FREEDOM DIVIDENDS

- Determine what step you're at and commit to moving forward in the steps to becoming financially free. Read the *7 Steps to Becoming Financially Free Workbook* and decide which method of budgeting will work best for you. Then get started on your financial plan!

Chapter 8

BREAKING FREE FROM DEBT

I recently heard it said that personal debt has given America three distinct classes of people: the haves, the have-nots, and the haven't-paid-for-what-they-haves! Isn't that so true? While funny on one level, it's also a sad commentary on the changes we've seen in our culture over the last several decades.

I think of my grandparents' generation. My grandfather built a successful lumber and coal business and didn't dream of going into debt for it, let alone for personal purchases. Debt just wasn't used by the average person back in the 1930s and 1940s. My parents also took a very conservative view when it came to borrowing money, again only relying on a mortgage to finance their home. Credit cards were paid off every month and they paid cash for major purchases such as cars and even college educations for the kids.

WHY DO AMERICANS HAVE SO MUCH DEBT?

During a radio program, a caller once asked me why I thought debt had become such a problem in America. I replied that in my opinion, it was a function of our fallen human nature, the increasingly consumer-driven society we live in, and the opportunity for businesses to make huge profits from the interest they can charge for lending money. Just take a look at the financial results of many of the country's largest companies and you'll find that their credit operations are often one of the largest contributors to their overall profit.

Scripture contains a number of references about debt that discourage its use, including Proverbs 22:7, which says, "The borrower is the slave of the lender." Habakkuk 2:6–7 warns, "Woe to him who heaps up what is not his own — for how long? — and loads himself with pledges! Will not your debtors suddenly arise, and those awake who will make you tremble? Then you will be booty for them." The Old Testament even speaks of debt at the national level. In Deuteronomy 28, the Lord speaks of a blessed nation being a lending nation, and a cursed nation being a borrowing nation. By and large, our grandparents' and parents' generations took this "scriptural sense" to heart and avoided debt. Unfortunately, we seem to have lost our fear of debt and instead it has become a financial drug that creates dependencies for millions of Americans.

There are types of debt for just about any situation you find yourself in, but the basic categories include the following:

- Credit cards
- Installment loans
- Automobile loans
- Student loans
- Home loans
- Home equity loans
- Cosigned loans

I'll cover issues related to home loans and home equity loans in Chapter 9, and student loans in Chapter 4. With the exception of home loans, student loans, and possibly cosigned loans, all of these forms of borrowing fall into the category of *consumer credit.* Let me give you a good rule of thumb when it comes to taking on debt: Never go into debt for anything that you don't expect to appreciate in value! While it's one thing to borrow prudently to purchase an appreciating asset, such as a home, investment property, or college education, Americans are borrowing billions of dollars to buy stuff that has no long-term value.

Let me be as clear as I can be: *If you want to reach true financial freedom, you need to eliminate **all** of your consumer credit.* It's as simple as that. If you currently have any consumer credit, you need to make a commitment to use the Accelerator Repayment Plan explained later in this chapter. It's your best opportunity to be free of financial bondage. But before I show you how to eliminate your debts with the Accelerator Repayment Plan, I want to share a few thoughts on each of these forms of debt.

To Credit Card or to Debit Card — That Is the Question

I have mixed emotions as to whether you should use a credit card, debit card, or neither. In general, my answer is to use what works for you, but you need to be totally honest with yourself. Too many people (about 20 percent of American households) get caught in the trap of only making the minimum payment that the finance company requires. This is ludicrous, because it means you're going to take at least five years to pay off last week's family outing to the pizza parlor! If you don't have the financial discipline to pay off a credit card in full every month, my recommendation is that you don't use them, and in fact, cut them up and cancel them. They're just too dangerous for you until your financial habits change.

When it comes to debit cards, people often think they're safer than credit cards since the funds are withdrawn directly from their bank account. However, many folks use overdraft privileges that are tied to their debit card. If they need a little extra cash, they go ahead with the purchase even though the money's not in the bank. The bank gladly allows it, since they'll make a profit from the interest charges. This is virtually the same thing as not paying your credit card off at the end of the month, and you'll pay heavily for it. So a debit card may work for you, but don't — I repeat *don't* — accept an overdraft capability on the account if you're going to use one.

The use of credit or debit cards requires a minor adjustment in tracking of expenses in the budget. Since your monthly credit-card bill or bank statement will have a large number of transactions that relate to different expenses, you'll need to summarize those transactions by the categories used in your budget. I use a numbering system (all grocery items are coded with 1; gasoline expenses get a 2, and so forth). When done coding, I total the amounts by category and transfer the account totals to our individual account register in order to update the budget.

If you don't have the confidence that you can manage either credit or debit cards responsibly, I recommend that you keep your system limited to cash and checks. An envelope-based system may be just what the doctor ordered.

The High Cost of Installment Sales

In almost all cases, installment sales make no sense. Installment sales typically require no down payment (or a minimal amount) and no payments for several months, followed by a certain number of "low" monthly payments.

The ability to purchase $5,000 or more in home furnishings with no cash out of pocket is too irresistible for many Americans, and companies are fully aware of this. The installment sale is a tool they use to boost revenues by selling to people who otherwise can't afford to purchase their products. The problems with installment sales include the following:

- The limited up-front cash commitment and low monthly payment entice customers to buy more than they can afford. If buying on installment becomes habitual, it most often leads to crushing levels of consumer debt with dire consequences for the family.
- Many financing plans carry interest rates of 20 percent or more. While no payment may be required for six months, in many cases interest begins accruing immediately — substantially increasing the cost of the purchase.
- With an installment sale, there is a presumption that you'll be able to meet the required future monthly obligations. Proverbs 22:26–27 reminds us, "Be not one of those who give pledges, who become surety for debts. If you have nothing with which to pay, why should your bed be taken from under you?"

In many cases, companies offering installment sales actually have higher prices than other companies because they have to cover losses associated with delinquent accounts. In addition to owing 20-percent interest, you may be paying substantially more for the item to begin with. One example comes to mind: A well-known retailer offered a set of cookware for $69.97 with payment in full at the time of sale, while another retailer offered the same cookware at $129.99. While few people paid cash upfront to purchase the cookware from the second company, many were enticed to use the payment plan of 18 installments at $11.49 each. If they had done the math, they would have realized that they were paying $206.82 for what they could have had for $69.97 at the first retailer.

So avoid the temptation of buying something you can't afford through an installment sale. Instead, save up so you can pay cash for the item. Who knows — after saving the money, you may realize that you really didn't want it anyway!

Automobile Loans

After housing, transportation is frequently the second highest expense in a budget. You can go a long way toward reducing your transportation costs by being smart about how you pay for a car. Remember my rule of thumb for taking on debt: You should only go into debt for an appreciating asset. Does a new car appreciate when you drive it off of the dealer's lot? Absolutely not! It depreciates 15 percent immediately since it's no longer new, and another 20 percent or so every year.

Consider purchasing slightly used cars with low mileage rather than buying them new. You avoid the 15-percent premium you would have to pay for a new car, and that adds up with today's car prices. Second, learn to save ahead for major purchases such as a vehicle so you can pay cash. (Remember Step Seven of the 7 Steps to Becoming Financially Free from the last chapter?) Why pay the banks all that interest? By the way, car companies *love* to lease you the vehicles. They know they make more money in the long run, since you're replacing the car fairly frequently. Pay cash for your car, keep it maintained, and drive it until either the cost or hassle of repairs isn't worth it any longer. Then sell it and pay cash for your next used car.

With that said, there may be times when financing a car makes sense. A good example is when an automobile manufacturer has a glut of inventory and develops incentive programs to reduce inventory levels. They may subsidize the purchase of a car by offering one-percent financing for three years. Assuming that you've already shopped around and the price is a good value relative to the cost of a slightly used car, the financing program can be an added benefit. In cases such as this it can make sense to leave the money in the bank, where it will be earning more interest than you're paying the finance company.

Cosigning — The Risks May Surprise You

The Book of Proverbs provides great insight into the issue of surety and cosigning. The basic principle is to not go there! Proverbs 6:1–5 says:

My son, if you have become surety for your neighbor, have given your pledge for a stranger; if you are snared in the utterance of your lips, caught in the words of your mouth; then do this, my son, and save yourself, for you have come into your neighbor's power: go, hasten, and importune your neighbor. Give your eyes no sleep, and your eyelids no slumber; save yourself like a gazelle from the hunter, like a bird from the hand of the fowler.

This verse doesn't suggest that there's anything morally wrong with cosigning, it just provides ample warning that the cosigner has to be aware that he or she has full responsibility for the debt.

If you've been asked to cosign a loan, ask yourself why the bank won't lend the money without your participation. Chances are the borrower is young and trying to establish credit, or the bank has reason to believe that the borrower is in over his or her head. If it's a young person trying to establish credit, there are better ways than requiring a cosigner (see section below on bankruptcy and restoring credit).

If you're still considering cosigning, you'll want to think through the following issues. When you cosign, be aware that the debt will be listed on your credit report, and in the event that the primary signer is late with payments, that information would be indicated on your report as well as his. There are cases where you may be taking on a greater responsibility than you think. For example, if a college student were to ask his parents to cosign on a credit card, the bank may be able to increase the credit limit without notice to the cosigner. That could be a recipe for disaster. Finally, if the primary signer fails to meet his obligation, the finance company will come to you for the balance, and you'll be bound to pay it.

TEN SIGNS OF DEBT DISTRESS

Here are 10 warning signs of debt distress that you can use to determine whether debt is causing problems.

- Do you argue with your spouse over bills? With half of marriages ending in divorce and finances playing a key role in these dissolutions, this should be a hot button for taking corrective action.

- Is an increasing percentage of your income being used to pay off debts? It's not uncommon for families to be spending several thousand dollars per year on interest charges that could otherwise be applied to basic needs. It's an interesting paradox to note that while families will spend 10 percent of their income on interest payments, they can only "afford" to give one percent for charitable causes. These numbers should be reversed.

- Are your credit cards at or near their credit limits? Do you keep applying for new cards to expand your limits?

- Are you only paying the minimum balances due on your credit card and other revolving credit accounts? Getting out of the minimum-payment mentality is a requirement for sound debt management.

- Are you chronically late in paying bills? Nearly half the country fails to pay bills on time, but barring exceptional situations, we have a responsibility to pay vendors in a timely manner.

- Do you borrow to purchase items that you used to pay cash for? This is an early warning sign of future problems.

- Do you put off medical or dental visits or necessary expenditures such as car maintenance because you don't have the money? Delaying true needs such as these often ends up causing much greater expenses in the long run.

- Would a job loss place you in immediate financial difficulty because of pre-existing credit-card debts? The high interest becomes impossible to manage with a major reduction in income.

- Are creditors calling you and threatening repossession or other forms of legal action? The stress from these calls and notices can cause all types of fissures to develop in a marriage relationship.

- Have you avoided adding up your total debt out of fear? Sidestepping the problem doesn't help to solve it.

If you answered yes to *any* of the above, your debts are placing you in financial bondage and you need to begin the Accelerator Repayment Plan today.

ELIMINATE YOUR DEBT — ACCELERATE IT!

The Accelerator Repayment Plan is a simple and straightforward approach to eliminating your consumer credit as rapidly as possible. How fast you eliminate your debt will partly depend on your circumstances, but it will also depend on how motivated you are to get out of debt and how committed you are to making the plan work.

Let's consider the example of Tom and Patty, who have three credit cards with balances totaling $10,000 and a car loan for $10,000. Their information is presented in the table below. The minimum monthly payments total $590, but that would take about four years to be debt free, and Tom and Patty would like to be debt free more quickly. After reviewing their budget, they have determined that they will allocate $800 each month for debt repayment. Rather than repaying the debts in four years, this plan eliminates them in less than two and a half years, and will save a bundle in interest charges. Let's review the seven steps that make up the Accelerator Repayment Plan:

1. Make a commitment to go no further into debt. If you can't muster the discipline to avoid purchases that you can't pay off immediately, cut your credit cards up.
2. Make sure that you have your $2,000 emergency fund set aside so that you'll be able to hold to your commitment when "surprises" occur.
3. Develop a realistic budget that includes a monthly amount dedicated to debt repayments. Your budget should balance after taking this monthly payment into account. As you're developing this plan to determine how much you can allocate to deficit repayment, use a debt calculator to consider different scenarios. As long as you know how much you owe and the average interest rate, you can play "what if" scenarios to see how long it would take to be debt-free at different payment levels. Visit www.VeritasFinancialMinistries.com to see how the Accelerator Repayment Plan can work in your situation.

4. The Accelerator Repayment Plan requires that you prioritize your debts for repayment. My preference, and the one that saves the most money, is to list your debts in order based on interest rate, with the highest-rate debt listed first. Some people prefer to list the smallest debt first, since it will be paid off relatively quickly, and they want to be able to celebrate a victory like that. Choose the method that will work best for you.

ACCELERATOR REPAYMENT PLAN EXAMPLE – TOM AND PATTY'S DEBTS					
Owed To	Balance	Rate	Minimum Monthly Payment	# Payments Based on Minimum Payment	# Payments Based on Accelerator Plan (a)
Visa	4,000	19%	120	48	14 payments at $330
Discover	2,000	17%	60	46	14 payments at $60 and 4 payments at $390
Master Card	4,000	14%	110	48	18 payments at $110 and 6 payments at $500
Car Loan	10,000	8%	300	38	24 payments at $300 and 5 payments at $800
Totals	20,000	NA	590	NA	NA

Every month you'll make the minimum payment required on each of the loans, except for the loan at the top of the repayment list. This is the one you're accelerating. In the example above, the minimum payment on the Visa bill is $120, but because Tom and Patty have committed $800 per month ($210 more than the minimum payment required on all loans), they can apply the additional $210 each month to the Visa card, for a total of $330. When the Visa bill is paid off, they'll continue applying $800 each month to the outstanding debts. With the Visa bill gone, they can zero in on the Discover Card. By adding the $330 payment they were making on the Visa to the $60 minimum payment they're making on the Discover Card, they have a new payment of $390. You can see how that amount will pay off the Discover Card in no time. You just repeat this process until the debts are eliminated!

5. You can reduce the time it will take to be debt-free even further by being creative about coming up with additional funds that can be applied to the Accelerator Repayment Plan. Consider having a garage sale or taking a temporary second job until the debts are eliminated. The plan will move as fast as you're committed to its moving.

6. Be accountable to someone. This can be your spouse, but if you don't have the discipline to stick with the plan on your own, bring in a friend, family member, or pastor to help you stay on track.

7. Set up a visual system to show your progress, such as a chart on the refrigerator that shows your declining debt balances. Depending on the circumstances, it's not uncommon for a debt repayment plan to take from one to five years, so a visual aid that tracks your progress can help you persevere.

Once you're debt free, think of the freedom of having $800 (or whatever amount you had allocated toward your debt) available each month for other purposes. You can pay your mortgage off early, save for retirement, start a college fund, and even have some fun!

WHAT YOU NEED TO KNOW ABOUT YOUR CREDIT REPORT AND YOUR FICO SCORE

Credit bureaus serve the business community by providing information about consumers, from where they work and live and how they pay their bills to whether they've been sued, arrested, or have filed for bankruptcy.

Practically speaking, before you'll be provided a consumer loan, granted insurance, or given a new credit card, your credit record will be reviewed.

While there are many local credit-rating organizations, there are only three major national credit bureaus, listed as follows:

- Equifax: www.equifax.com
- Experian: www.experian.com
- Trans Union: www.transunion.com

It's important for you to keep up-to-date with the information the credit bureaus are maintaining. Even if you think your credit is stellar, errors are fairly common, and these can impact how businesses make decisions regarding the issuance of credit. The best way to obtain the information the credit bureaus are sharing with others is to periodically request a copy of your credit record. Federal law allows consumers to request a free copy of their report from each of the bureaus every 12 months, and you should take advantage of this. The official site to obtain a free credit report is www.annualcreditreport.com.

Once you receive your report, you'll find that it includes key information for each of your credit accounts. This will include the creditor, type of account, terms of credit, amount of the original debt, credit limit, and the current balance outstanding. There will also be a payment profile documenting whether you have been timely in meeting your obligations.

If you notice a problem, document your dispute in writing and send it to the appropriate bureau. The letter should include your complete name and address, clear identification and explanations of each item disputed, and a request to delete or correct the items in question. It would also be a good idea to provide a copy of the agency's credit report with the disputed items highlighted. You should also send copies of records (not originals) that support your position. Send your dispute letter by certified mail, return receipt requested, so that you have proof of delivery. Also, keep a copy of your letter for your own file.

Once the bureau receives your request, they're obliged to investigate the item (usually within 30 days) by presenting to their information source the evidence you submit. The source must review your information and report its findings to the bureau. The credit bureau also has the responsibility of notifying other national bureaus of any incorrect information they previously supplied. If the results of the investigation show that errors were contained in your credit report, the bureau must remove the incorrect information within a reasonable time frame.

Upon completion of the investigation, you're entitled to receive a report summarizing the results as well as a revised copy of your credit report if the investigation results in a change. Upon request, the agency is also obligated to notify anyone who has recently received your report of the corrections.

If the investigation shows that the report was accurate, the bureau has no obligation to remove the information from your file until it is outdated. Regular credit information can stay on your report for up to 7 years, while bankruptcy information can be included for up to 10 years. Even if the problematic credit information is accurate, you do have a right to add a brief statement to your file, which the bureau must normally include in future reports. For more information on your rights as a consumer, review the *Federal Fair Credit Reporting Act* at www.ftc.gov.

While it has always been important to keep up-to-date with the information contained in your credit reports, it has become even more important with the proliferation of identity theft. By ordering a free copy of your credit report from one of the three bureaus every four months, you'll be able to stay on top of any questionable activity. For additional information on how to avoid identity theft and what to do in the event it happens to you, go to www.consumer.gov/idtheft/.

FICO is an acronym for Fair Isaac Companies, which developed the FICO credit scoring system. Maintaining a good FICO score is simply a function of managing your credit well, which means paying your bills on time and paying off your credit cards each month. Most lenders rely on this system when making loans. The scoring ranges from 300 to 850, and these scores will impact whether you can obtain a loan, as well as the interest rate you'll be paying. For example, www.myFICO.com uses the following table to illustrate the impact your FICO score can have on the interest rate and monthly payment you'd owe on a 30-year fixed mortgage of $150,000:

FICO Score	Interest Rate	Monthly Payment
760–850	5.65	865
700–759	5.86	886
680–699	6.04	903
660–679	6.25	924
640–659	6.68	966
620–639	7.23	1,021

HOW A CREDIT COUNSELING SERVICE CAN HELP YOU

I'm an advocate of taking charge of your own credit problems and developing your own debt repayment plan using the Accelerator Repayment Plan. However, if you can't even manage the *minimum* payments required by the creditors and you want someone to help you along the way, one solution is to work with a credit counseling service. Remember that burying your head in the sand and hoping the problem will go away is the worst thing you can do. Whether or not you use a credit counseling service, make sure you communicate with your lender. In most cases, they'll be much more willing to work with you if you're open about your problem.

You'll want to use caution in locating the right service for you, and complete due diligence before using their program. If you open the yellow pages under "credit," you'll find a multitude of credit counseling services. Some of these will be for-profit organizations, while others have non-profit status. Some will "cherry pick" the loans they will assist you with. You'll want to find an organization that will deal with *all* of your consumer credit. Many local agencies are affiliated with the National Foundation for Consumer Credit (www.nfcc.org), which was founded in 1951. These agencies have developed a good reputation over the years.

If you go to an agency affiliated with NFCC, you can expect them to offer free budget and credit counseling. They also offer debt management plans. For a relatively modest fee, they will set up a consolidation loan.

This results in you making *one* payment to them. They then make disbursements to your creditors based on a negotiated schedule. Because they have established relationships with lenders, they will frequently be able to negotiate favorable repayment terms, such as a reduction in your overall interest rate.

BANKRUPTCY AND RESTORATION OF CREDIT

People often ask whether it's appropriate to declare bankruptcy as a Catholic. The answer is that it truly depends. We are called to responsibly manage the resources the Lord has given us, and this means keeping the promises we make (CCC 2410) — including the repaying of our debts (CCC 2411). We need to take our debt obligations (such as credit-card debt) seriously! On the other hand, it's clear that circumstances in life can overwhelm people and leave them in untenable financial situations. A good example of this would be when someone incurs very large hospital bills and doesn't have medical insurance. In fact, medical bills are one of the leading causes of personal bankruptcy in America today. In cases such as this, it's clear that there needs to be a mechanism to relieve the financial strain. We read in Deuteronomy 15:1–11 that the Lord provided a way for debts to be released every seven years, and our bankruptcy system is the mechanism we have in place today for that purpose.

Bankruptcy should only become a consideration if you're in a position where you're unable to meet your true needs and those of your family. Before you can make such an assessment, you need to prepare a budget that lays out your essential expenses and the amount you can reasonably apply to debt repayment. If the creditors are willing to work with you and accept a repayment schedule that allows you to meet your ongoing needs, it would be best to follow such a repayment schedule. If, on the other hand, creditors require a level of resources that will not allow you to meet your needs, then seeking relief through bankruptcy is a viable option. If you feel bankruptcy is your only recourse, it's important that you seek professional legal counsel.

Another important principle when it comes to bankruptcy is the concept of restitution. While a bankruptcy discharge may eliminate your debts legally, remember that there is merit in repaying those debts from a moral vantage point if you someday find yourself in a position to do so (CCC 2412).

People who go through bankruptcy or who have otherwise developed a poor credit record often wonder how they can go about restoring their credit. Here are some commonsense tips. First of all, make sure that you have a savings and checking account, and manage the checking account well over time (no bad checks). This will show that you're being financially responsible. If you feel you're ready to properly manage credit cards, you can begin by obtaining a "secured" credit card against your savings account for a specified dollar amount. This can be an effective way to establish credit without the use of a cosigner.

 FREEDOM DIVIDENDS

- If you have *any* consumer credit, commit to eliminating your debt as fast as you can using the Accelerator Repayment Plan of debt reduction. Be creative and aggressive about finding additional funds to reduce the payback period.
- Obtain and review a free annual copy of your credit report from each of the three credit bureaus.

Chapter 9

HOME SWEET HOME

I remember spending many a Saturday driving around looking for just the right house in the perfect neighborhood when my wife and I were ready to buy our first home. It was an exciting time! We were starting our family and were looking forward to "having our own place." Buying and owning a house will probably be one of the biggest monetary decisions you make in life. In this chapter, I want to cover a number of issues related to home ownership. These are big-picture decisions that, if made wisely, will lead to financial freedom . . . but if disregarded, can lead to major money headaches.

HOUSE RICH . . . OR HOUSE POOR?

I recently visited with an attorney and his wife who were having difficulties due to money issues in their marriage. Their problems were in some ways different than those of the average American couple, since he earned a solid six-figure income and they lived in a $1.5 million dollar home. Yet in other ways, they were struggling with exactly the same challenges that so many Americans face. They had purchased more home than they could afford, and were having a hard time making room for other important priorities.

While it may be difficult to feel sorry for this couple, their situation highlights one of the biggest causes of financial pressure today. People do all they can to buy as much house as possible, but find they're "house rich," to the detriment of the other goals they have in life. They're unable to afford a good Catholic education for their children, they forego important insurance needs, they certainly aren't saving or tithing, and they often find themselves using credit cards to meet their other needs.

In our search for the American Dream, we can let our eyes and emotions run way ahead of our available resources. The greatest advice I can offer in this chapter is *make sure you don't fall into the trap of buying more house than you can afford.* In Luke 14:28–29, Jesus tells us, "For which of you, desiring to build a tower, does not first sit down and count the cost, whether he has enough to complete it? Otherwise, when he has laid a foundation, and is not able to finish, all who see it begin to mock him, saying, 'This man began to build, and was not able to finish.'"

You'll recall that my guideline budget suggests that all housing costs (including payment, property taxes, insurance, utilities, telephone, gardening, and improvements) be limited to about 30 percent of your gross income. This can be a real challenge with the current cost of housing, especially at lower income levels. It's not uncommon for me to counsel folks where total housing costs are between 40 to 50 percent of their gross income. While the 30 percent figure is only a guideline, and there is room for some flexibility, when you get to the 40 to 50 percent range, it becomes virtually impossible to balance out your other priorities appropriately. Something has to give.

Keeping your housing costs within a level you can truly afford will probably mean buying less house than you are dreaming of. My parents started very simple and often shared the story of renting their first "home." At the time, my oldest brother was a toddler and my oldest sister was a newborn. The house had one bedroom and my brother slept in the bedroom with my parents, while my sister slept in a basket on top of the washing machine! My parents understood the importance of keeping overall housing costs within their means. Too many young people want to start where their parents have ended up rather than where the parents started.

Another example comes to mind. Some neighbors of ours were considering whether to move to a larger home. They were in a position to afford it, but had other priorities they felt were more important. For one, they wanted to build family togetherness by going on more frequent vacations and outings. So they talked the two options over with their children. Would the kids rather live in a bigger home, or would they prefer to take nicer vacations as a family and be able to pursue additional hobbies that they wouldn't be able to afford if they moved to a more expensive house? To the delight of the parents, the kids chose to stay put and spend the extra money on more opportunities for the family to do things together.

Don't get me wrong. Housing has proven to be a sound investment over a long period of time, and there's no reason to think that over the long run it won't continue to be a good investment and perhaps one of your largest assets. But if you fall into the trap of buying as much as you can, especially with the more risky types of loans available today, you can expect that it will create a good deal of tension in the home — and that's not good for the family.

What should you do if you already own a home that's sapping your checkbook dry? I suggest you take a hard look at your budget and consider whether you'll be in a position to adequately meet your other obligations over the next five years or so. Maybe you're confident that your income will increase sufficiently over the next few years to bring your situation back into balance. But be realistic about it. If you can't see how a proper balance will be achieved, the healthiest decision may be to downsize.

RENT OR BUY?

If you aren't yet a homeowner but expect to be one in the next few years — maybe you're engaged to be married — you have a golden opportunity to get started on the right foot. Here are a number of ideas to consider.

When comparing renting an apartment and buying a house, many would have the same response: "Why waste money on rent when I can buy a house that I'll own? Besides, I can deduct the mortgage interest!" At first glance these arguments make sense. What is often overlooked, however, are the substantial costs of home ownership, including the following:

- Purchase costs, such as a down payment and the expense of obtaining a mortgage, including points, title fees, and loan-processing charges.

- Ongoing costs of ownership — property taxes, insurance, utilities, gardening, and other expenses that increase the cost of home ownership in relation to the rental charge of an apartment.
- Selling costs, including 3 to 6 percent of the sales price as a commission (unless you sell it yourself or work out a special arrangement with your realtor) and other selling expenses.

In addition to the costs noted above, it normally takes quite some time to build equity in your home because most of your monthly payment in the early years of a mortgage is applied to interest. As an example, if you take out a 30-year mortgage for $200,000 at a 6 percent interest rate, you'll pay almost $12,000 in interest out of a total of $14,400 in payments during the 12 months alone.

Most people in their early 20s find themselves in a rapidly changing environment — from finishing college and starting a career to getting married and starting a family. These life changes frequently result in multiple moves, which, based on the costs noted above would be very expensive in the event that you owned a home.

By taking all of these factors into account, most young couples would be better off keeping their initial housing expenses low and maintaining the flexibility that renting provides. Once you have settled in your career and have a higher degree of certainty that you'll remain in one location for a longer period of time, it would make sense to start looking for a home. As Proverbs 24:27 reminds us, "Prepare your work outside, get everything ready for you in the field; and after that build your house."

Here are a few questions you can use to determine when purchasing a home makes sense:

- Are you reasonably sure that you'll live in the home for at least five years?
- Do you have a stable job?
- Do you have the means to make an adequate down payment (preferably 20 percent)?
- Are you living on a budget?

- Are you planning in such a way that provides the maximum opportunity for a full-time parent to nurture the children at home when that day arrives?

TAKING THE PLUNGE

Once you've determined that you're ready to buy a home, what are the steps you should take to make a good decision? The first thing you need to do is to complete what is called a "pro-forma" budget. This is simply a forecasted budget for the first year you own your home. It would include your anticipated house payment, property taxes, insurance, utilities, gardening, and improvement costs that you expect to incur on an annual basis along with all your other regular bills. Especially if the house is older, you'll want to factor in a reasonable amount for ongoing repairs, such as the replacement of a roof. That way, when you visit the bank, you'll be able to tell them how much you can afford rather than letting them tell you what you can qualify for. Remember, the more money they loan you, the more money they make. Most banks use a formula that leads to a debt burden you'll find oppressive (40 percent of gross income allowed for all debt payments).

Another tip to keep in mind when you're searching for a loan is that most buyers fall into the trap of focusing on keeping the monthly payment as low as possible rather than on the amount they're borrowing and how long they'll be in debt. This leads to creative financing that keeps you in debt for a lot longer than you should be and makes you pay a lot more interest than is wise. I'll talk about this more in a moment.

You've heard the real estate mantra before, "Location, location, location." Along with determining ahead of time how much house you can afford, and making smart financing decisions, this is one of the most important factors to consider when buying a home. It will impact how happy you will be while living there and your ability to sell in the event you choose to move in the future. Is the location a desirable one? Will your commute to work be reasonable? Are you within a desirable proximity to family? Is the regional economy growing and does it appear well-poised for the future? Are the schools in the neighborhood highly regarded? Are the other houses in the neighborhood well-maintained? Are the neighbors friendly? Are there any zoning issues that would be of concern (such as a retail center being built on the open lot behind you)? Go door-to-door and visit with potential new neighbors. It will be well worth your time. Make sure the home receives a thorough inspection. You should do much of this on your own, but it would also be a good idea to bring in a professional whom you trust. Structural problems found after the purchase is complete can be a major headache and very expensive.

Before making an offer, be sure you have a good understanding of the recent sales activity in the neighborhood. Your real estate agent will be able to provide you with a Comparable Market Analysis, which shows pricing information for homes currently on the market and those recently sold. It also provides summary information about those homes, including overall size, number of rooms, and so on. This information helps the buyer and seller understand what's reasonable when it comes to reaching agreement on a price.

SMART (AND DUMB) FINANCING

The high cost of housing has led lenders to develop very creative forms of financing that, while successful at getting someone into a home, don't really consider the long-term well-being of the buyer. These creative forms of financing include 100 percent financing, interest-only loans, loans with balloon payments, and loans that extend beyond the traditional 30-year variety. Each of these types of loans has the objective of lowering the current monthly payment, but at the cost of maximizing the amount of interest the borrower will pay and the length of time they will be in debt.

Call me old fashioned, but I'm a believer in making a substantial down payment (20 percent is a good objective) and in obtaining a loan that allows one to own their home outright as soon as practical. I encourage the use of 15-year loans, or at least committing to prepaying a typical 30-year loan over 15 years. Here's why:

Once someone buys their first home, they end up being surprised at how little equity they initially build, assuming stable prices. What they don't realize is that very little of the monthly payment in the early years of a 30-year mortgage reduces the actual loan, because most of it is being applied to interest. As I mentioned earlier, for a 30-year loan of $200,000 at a 6 percent interest rate, only $2,400 goes toward the principle balance during the first year, out of total payments of more than $14,000. Your friendly bank appreciates the business!

The most effective way to build the equity in your home more rapidly is to either take out a 15-year loan or "prepay" your mortgage. An added benefit to a 15-year loan is that interest rates will normally be about one-half of a percentage point less than similar 30-year loans. Based on the figures presented in the following table, the monthly payment required for the 30-year loan is $1,199.10. But if you took out a 15-year loan, your payment would only increase by $435.07 for a total payment of $1,634.17. You'd end up saving nearly $140,000 in interest!

EXHIBIT 1 — EFFECT OF PREPAYING MORTGAGE		
	30 Year Loan	**15 Year Loan**
Original Loan Amount	$200,000	$200,000
Interest Rate	6.0%	5.5%
Monthly Payment	$1,199.10	$1,634.17
Difference in Monthly Payments	N/A	$435.07
Total Cash Paid During Term of Loan	$431,676.00	$294,150.60
Interest Saved	N/A	$137,525.40

Some financial planners recommend paying your loan off over the standard 30-year period and investing the difference. While this can theoretically make sense, as it does take advantage of compound earnings and the time value of money, it depends on whether you will actually save the difference every month, and whether you can obtain a consistent return at least equal to the interest rate on your mortgage. My experience tells me that very few people have the discipline to save that discretionary income every month. Instead they end up spending it on regular bills. They really need that tangible goal of owning their house in 15 years along with the forced discipline the 15-year loan gives them in order to stick with the plan. An added benefit of paying your loan off over 15-20 years is that when your children reach college age, the funds that were going to the mortgage will be freed up for educational needs. Financially speaking, you'd be well served to both save consistently and prepay your mortgage.

While it may seem difficult to come up with the extra money required, a can-do attitude combined with proper planning makes it possible. Most people find that as the years go by, increases in income disappear as a result of increased discretionary spending. Rather than wasting these increases, I recommend a large portion (say 30 percent) be applied as additional payments on your home loan. With the house paid off in 15 years, you'll have the freedom to use the extra funds for other priorities, such as college education for the children or retirement savings.

Even if you can't afford to increase your payment to a level that would cut the length of your loan in half, I would encourage you to start with some amount — even if only $100 per month. As your income grows, the discipline will be in place to make a wise decision on how the increase should be allocated.

WHEN DOES REFINANCING MAKE SENSE?

When current interest rates are lower than those tied to your mortgage, refinancing can save you money in the long run, yet you'll have to pay certain fees to achieve these savings, such as points, processing fees, title charges, escrow fees, loan prepayment penalties (if any), and other potential costs. As a rule of thumb, if you can reduce your interest rate by two percent and expect to live in the home for at least two years, refinancing may be a good idea.

Just as it is for any other major purchase, it will be a good idea to seek information from a number of lenders or brokers to be confident that you're getting the best deal. Contact about 10 lenders to obtain basic rate and cost information, and to get a feel for how comfortable you are working with them. A simple way to get started is to use comparison sites on the Internet (such as www.eloan.com and www.bankrate.com). Keep in mind the importance of comparing apples to apples. You might find one lender offering a low interest rate with higher up-front costs, and another lender with a higher rate and lower costs. Once you've run through the numbers, you can narrow the list down to the top three. Ask each of them to give you a solid proposal for refinancing with a complete estimate of closing costs so you can make a final decision.

Here's one trap to avoid. Let's say your current monthly payment is $1,000 and it's expected to drop to $800 after refinancing. Some of this $200 in savings comes from the reduction in interest rates, but some of it probably comes from extending the payback period of your loan. In other words, if you bought your home 10 years ago and financed it with a 30-year mortgage, you now have 20 years remaining on the loan. Yet, if you refinance with a 30-year loan today, your mortgage won't be paid off until 10 years later than your current loan. Much of the decline in your monthly payment is due to the extension of the loan for an additional 10 years. While it may feel good today to have a lower monthly payment, in the long run it'll cost you more because of the interest you'll pay for those additional 10 years. The solution is to obtain a loan with the same payoff date as your current loan (which may be difficult to do) or to refinance with a standard 15- or 30-year loan where you make additional principal payments each month in order to maintain a consistent payoff schedule.

WHAT ABOUT HOME EQUITY LOANS?

A recent study released by the Federal Reserve noted that $600 billion was extracted from home equity in 2004. This was three times the level taken out in 2000. As I write this, the nation has experienced a record run-up in real estate prices. In the San Diego area, where we live, prices have doubled over the last four to five years. With that level of price appreciation, it can be incredibly tempting to use the equity for any number of reasons, including paying off credit card debt, making home improvements, and even as a source of funds for general expenses.

At first glance, using the equity in your home to eliminate credit card debts seems like a great idea. After all, the required monthly payment drops by a significant amount and you even get a tax deduction! However, this solution is in essence a swapping of short-term debt for long-term debt, and as a result, is *not* an effective debt-repayment strategy. The attractiveness of the lower monthly payment that comes from a home equity loan or refinancing is blinding you to the fact that, rather than paying interest for 2 or 3 years under the Accelerated Repayment Plan, you'll be paying interest for up to 30 years. Consider the example of a couple with $20,000 in credit card debt who are trying to decide if they ought to use the equity in their home to consolidate their debt. Assuming an interest rate on the credit cards of 10 percent (keeping the rate low by rolling balances to cards with introductory offers), they'd incur about $3,200 in interest charges over 3 years, whereas interest on a 30-year loan at 7 percent totals about $28,000! Why would anyone want to pay $25,000 more in interest?

Another key reason I recommend creating an accelerated debt repayment plan without using the equity in your home is that, for most people, the accumulation of credit card debt is a symptom rather than the root of the problem. I frequently counsel folks who have already taken out a home equity loan, yet find themselves facing the dilemma of massive new credit card debts. What happened? Because they don't have a budget, they find themselves continually spending more than they can afford and making it up with their credit cards. For a short period of time after their initial consolidation (typically six months to a year), their life returned to normal and it seemed as though the problem was solved. Unfortunately, they never changed their basic spending habits, and slowly but surely, the credit card balances once again began to creep up. Eventually, the minimum payment reached a point where they couldn't meet their obligations again. Only now they had already lost the equity in their home. I recognize that every situation is unique, but I encourage you to develop a debt-repayment strategy that doesn't rely on the hard-earned equity you've built up in your home.

What about using the equity in your home for home improvements or general expenses? Remember my general rule of thumb not to go into debt for anything that doesn't appreciate in value. Some will argue that certain types of home improvements will cause an increase in value beyond the amount spent, but once you take into account the interest you pay on the loan, this will be true in very few instances. Save up before moving ahead with improvements if at all possible. I understand there may be instances where a growing family requires additional space *now*, and adding on to the existing home offers the best alternative, even if a loan is required. If you have to go this route, develop a plan to retire the loan as quickly as possible.

 FREEDOM DIVIDENDS

- If you're in the market to purchase a home, take the time to complete a "pro forma" budget for the first year of home ownership before you do anything else. Make sure you'll be able to meet your other priorities in a balanced way.
- Don't fall into the trap of using the "creative" financing that is available, such as no-interest loans, balloon-payment loans, and loans that are for 100 percent of the value of the home. Look for ways to shorten the amount of time you'll owe a mortgage on your home from 30-plus years to no more than 15 or 20.

Chapter 10

SMART SPENDING — HABITS OF THE FINANCIALLY FREE

*M*any think of stewardship in relation to how much they give, and that is an important part of being a "Steward of Providence." Just as important, though, is what we do with the rest of our money. It's a funny thing, but as people apply the principles in this book, they often become more generous, yet find that the remaining 90 percent goes further than the 100 percent they had before. How is that? It's because now they're giving in the context of an overall financial plan, and in the process they become wiser in terms of how they spend their money. Here are a number of smart spending habits to develop that will help you become financially free.

SPEND ACCORDING TO YOUR PLAN

One of the most important habits you can develop is to spend according to your budget. That means you need to have a plan in the first place! Impulse buying is an enemy of financial freedom, especially when it relates to big purchases, or even when smaller purchases turn into regular habits — do I hear anyone saying "Latté"? Again, let's strive for balance in this area. It's a good thing to budget an allowance for you and your spouse that you can spend without having to give an account, a so-called "impulse" budget. That type of impulse buying isn't the problem. The problem arises when spending based on impulse is the norm rather than the exception. Those of you with children know how often they have difficulty controlling their emotions when it comes to wanting something. Just consider little Johnny in the grocery-store cart when mom rolls past the candy bars at the checkout counter!

Fortunately, we do tend to mature a bit as we get older, but we may still find it difficult to control our spending at times. We all have a little bit of "kid" in us, don't we? We'd rather not think ahead about the consequences of our impulse buying. But let me tell you something: Chances are that how you spend your money will be a greater determining factor in your becoming financially free than how much you make in the first place.

Another factor to consider when laying out your spending plans is to learn to anticipate your needs. Seasonal purchases are a great example. If you know you'll need a winter coat, don't wait until the first frost to buy it. You'll pay a premium, whereas you could have spent much less by purchasing it as part of the prior year's winter closeout sale.

One of the great disciplines the Church offers that can help you master impulse buying is fasting, typically understood as the taking of only one full meal in a day. Section 2043 of the *Catechism of the Catholic Church* says that fasting "helps us acquire mastery over our instincts and freedom of heart." Learning to acquire self-mastery is just what we need! While fasting is a requirement on Ash Wednesday and Good Friday, there's no reason we can't use this powerful tool more frequently. I know a number of people who choose to fast in some manner on a weekly basis. You'll find that your character and will are strengthened, and that you make better spending decisions.

COMPARISON SHOP

Another spending habit to develop is to become a comparison shopper. This is important for major purchases that occur only once in a while as well as for day-to-day expenses that add up over the course of a year. Major purchases include such things as your home, automobiles, education, home improvements, and various insurance policies. Each of these items has a relatively high cost, so saving 10 to 20 percent or more becomes a substantial sum very quickly. You'll always want to take the time to gather adequate information about these bigger items so you'll be confident that you're getting a good deal.

Let me give you an example from a few years back when I bought a new car.

After settling on the vehicle that made sense for us, I utilized the online (and free) services of www.kelleybluebook.com. I also purchased a new-car price report for our desired model from *Consumer Reports* for a cost of $12. This report was invaluable because it provided not only the dealer invoice price, but also the Consumer Reports Wholesale Price. This provided the amount of any rebates the dealer expected to receive from the manufacturer. The website of the manufacturer came in handy as well, since it showed me the dealers that were within a reasonable range of our hometown. I e-mailed the closest 15 dealers with the details of the car I wanted, including options. Four dealers responded, and one of them submitted what, in my view, was a fair offer. I then made an appointment with the dealer and we were done with the paperwork in less than an hour. It was nearly painless, and I'm confident that I saved a few thousand dollars compared to what I would have spent had I not completed the background work.

When it comes to major purchases, the value in comparison shopping is clear. However, people often let their guard down when it comes to smaller items. Examples include groceries, clothing, meals out, entertainment and recreation, and gas for the cars. Even though these purchases are relatively small each time you make them, the cumulative amount ends up being substantial over the course of a year and can have a detrimental effect on the bottom line of an annual budget. You'll want to be a comparison shopper on these things, too.

For those of you interested in making your dollars go further, Amy Dacyczyn has become one of the true experts at living a frugal lifestyle. While not all of her suggestions will be for everyone, I highly recommend her book *The Tightwad Gazette,* which is an invaluable resource for those families wanting to stretch their resources. Amy developed what she called a "price book," which can be a great saving tool for your family. The price book was originally created to monitor grocery costs, but you can use it effectively for other items you purchase regularly as well. It includes space for you to note the price per unit you pay for the items at various stores at different times. As a result, you end up knowing the lowest price you've paid for that item in the past and whether the store is presently offering a good deal. If it is, you can stock up with confidence. This kind of smart shopping will allow your hard-earned dollars to stretch. (See the *7 Steps to Becoming Financially Free Workbook* for a sample price list that can also be used for this purpose.)

It's easy to get excited over the savings offered by grocery coupons, and they can provide valuable savings. But that's not always the case. If you use coupons blindly, you'll fall into the trap of paying more to buy well-known brands, and may not recognize that another store may offer the item at a lower everyday price than the store with the coupon. The only way you can truly know a good deal is to track the prices of the items you buy most often, and the best way to do that is with the price book. I know in our case, Chelsey has found that different stores tend to consistently offer lower prices on certain items. One store offers a great deal on dairy products, and another is best when it comes to produce. We tend to rotate among about four stores in our area to maximize our savings.

THE "BRANDING" OF AMERICA

Madison Avenue works overtime creating desires within you so you'll spend your hard-earned cash. According to one private investment firm's forecast, over $200 billion is now being spent on advertising each year[35]. There's nothing wrong with much of the advertising out there — a company needs to make you aware of its product and the benefits it can bring you. Brands become trusted for certain qualities in their products, and it's good for companies to promote that. Many of the ad campaigns are clean and filled with good humor.

Advertising becomes a problem when you end up buying things you don't need or can't afford, and worse, when you chase after images presented in the advertisement — especially if the imagery is contrary to the values of our faith. Let me give you an example: I recently came across an advertising insert in a well-respected national daily paper. The insert was for an upscale car and ran 16 pages. Like many ads today, it appealed to our baser senses by tying a beautiful woman and the car together. The message was clear: get the car and you get the woman. It's a seductive statement that promotes the idea that life can be lived for self, regardless of moral and financial considerations, because "you deserve it."

These types of ads are not harmless. They create emotional responses in us that aren't always based on the most virtuous thoughts. When we buy something because of advertising like this, we may be motivated by ego, and falling into that trap can be expensive — both monetarily and spiritually. So recognize advertising for what it is. Don't make purchases based on images, but rather on your needs and the merits of the product itself.

DON'T BE AFRAID TO BUY ITEMS "SLIGHTLY USED"

A great way to stretch your resources is to purchase gently used items. These can include cars, home furnishings, tools, and clothing. It's true that you won't get that "special" smell that comes with many new items, nor will you be able to be as selective about the style you want. But let me ask you this: After a year of owning something, hasn't the newness disappeared and the desire for a particular color gone away? By locking yourself in to a particular brand, style, and color too early, you end up losing a lot of your bargaining power.

There are a number of places to consider when making used purchases, including estate and garage sales as well as flea markets. One of the best ways to find what you're looking for, though, is to let your family and friends know what you're seeking. You'll be surprised at how often someone in your circle of friends will have just what you want, and be happy to have you take it off their hands. We know of a family that put out the word that they wanted to buy a piano at a good price. Within six months, two free pianos were offered to the family, each an older model, but lovingly maintained.

Even if the item isn't exactly what you wanted, you may still find it to be a good bargain. If you get it for an especially good price, you may be able to make use of it in the interim — perhaps even eventually selling it for more than you bought it — then purchase the item that you really wanted. This whole fascination with "trading" is part of what has made eBay a household name, and it could work for you, too.

SLEEP ON THE BIG DECISIONS

You all know the symptoms: the adrenaline rush; then the rationalizing points you make to yourself or your spouse about why you need the new car, dining-room set, boat, bicycle, golf clubs, or whatever else it is you're considering; and that little voice telling you why it's so important that you get it today. When the buying bug hits, it hits hard, and none of us is immune!

When you have the buying bug for a big-ticket item, that's when you're most vulnerable as a consumer. You become willing to throw out all the good spending habits I've just covered. *Just this once,* you say, *it doesn't matter that the item isn't in my budget.* You've settled on a particular brand, aren't in a mood to take the time to comparison shop, and won't consider waiting to see if you can get what you want used for a fraction of the price. I know because I've been there!

I hope that as you apply the principles in this book, you'll have fewer instances of the buying bug. But my guess is that you'll never completely get rid of it. So make the commitment that when it hits, you'll take the time to sleep on the buying decision. Take another look at your budget and consider whether the purchase fits into your current plan. Even if it does fit, ask yourself if it's the best use of your funds at the present time — because once that money is gone, it's gone.

ANSWERING YOUR QUESTIONS ON INSURANCE

While you won't find insurance in sacred Scripture, per se, you will find teaching that encourages us to make effective plans to meet the needs of our family. For example, 1 Timothy 5:8 says, "If anyone does not provide for his own relatives and especially for members of his immediate family, he has denied the faith; he is worse than an unbeliever." In biblical times, society was based on an agrarian economy, with land being passed on from generation to generation. This acted as the equivalent of an insurance policy. With the shift to an industrial and information-based economy, another form of safeguard became necessary. Insurance has filled this need, and is an appropriate tool that helps us fulfill the instruction given in 1 Timothy.

There are five primary types of insurance coverage that are important for us to deal with, including health, home, auto, life, and disability. There isn't room here for an exhaustive review, so I'll just touch on some basics. If you'd like to dig deeper into the insurance topic, I recommend reading *Insurance for Dummies*. While I'm an advocate of reasonable insurance coverage, don't fall into the trap of overspending in this area. Remember that insurance is meant to minimize your risk of a catastrophic loss, not pay for all of life's emergencies. By keeping that in mind, you'll select levels of insurance that won't bankrupt your budget.

Health Insurance

Health insurance is something I advocate for everyone. Crushing medical-care costs represent one of the primary reasons that people declare bankruptcy. If you're confronted with a serious accident or illness in your family and don't have insurance, it doesn't take long for the bills to mount into the hundreds of thousands of dollars. The prudent person will cover for this possibility with an appropriate level of health insurance.

Health insurance policies have become more and more expensive over the years, and today, it can cost over $10,000 per year to pay the full premiums on a typical family plan. Fortunately, health insurance continues to be one of the most substantial benefits employers offer, although many are requiring employees to shoulder more of the cost burden. So when you're considering various job options, make sure you factor in the level of health-care benefits provided by your potential employer. If your employer doesn't offer coverage, it's still important for you to obtain a catastrophic policy that will come with a high deductible, but will at least cap your losses at a predetermined amount.

Home and Auto Insurance

Basic home and auto insurance policies are often required either by your state or lender, but you certainly have the option to carry higher levels than required, and in most cases that's a prudent thing to do. Here are some things to look for in these policies:

- With your auto insurance, insure adequately in the event you hurt someone and are held liable for injuries. I would insure for at least $100,000 per person and $300,000 per occurrence.

- Similarly, part of your auto insurance will be for damage you cause to someone's property. With the increasing cost of cars, I recommend a level of $50,000 for this component.
- One of the more expensive coverages for auto insurance is collision, which pays for damage to your car. It's smart to select the highest deductible you're comfortable with in order to save on your premium. You may also consider dropping the coverage on older cars, since the benefit will be limited to the car's cash value.
- Just as with your auto policies, consider raising your deductible on your home insurance as a way to lower your premium.
- Check your home insurance policy to verify whether certain types of disasters are covered, such as floods and earthquakes. It's also important that you obtain a policy with adequate "replacement coverage" given the increasing cost of housing. Make sure to take photos of the contents of the home, including furnishings and valuables and keep the pictures in a safe place in order to have proof of ownership.

I remember the story of a woman who had been making a six-figure income working with a very large company . She wanted to leave her work to become a teacher, even though it would mean a substantial reduction in pay. After discussing it with her husband, she went ahead and made the change, but one of the ways they made the budget work was to cancel their home insurance. Given that their home was their largest asset, this decision left them in a very vulnerable position. They would have been wiser to look at other areas in the budget to make adjustments rather than eliminating the insurance on their home. Don't cut corners like this or you may end up regretting it.

Life Insurance

Life insurance can be complicated, but by understanding a few basics, you'll be able to make good decisions. First of all, life insurance becomes a necessity in my view once you have children. As a father of seven, I realize that my family is dependent on my ability to generate an income over a long period of time — probably 40 years given the age range of our kids! It's my responsibility to do the best I can to provide for them in the event that I die earlier than anticipated.

There are basically two types of life insurance policies: term insurance and everything else. Term insurance simply provides a fixed payment upon death. Other forms of life insurance, including whole life, universal life, and variable life, offer a combination of insurance and tax-deferred savings benefits. In my view, term insurance is the most appropriate type for the vast majority of families. It's the most affordable option and accomplishes the basics of what you're looking for — namely, that your family will receive a fixed sum of insurance proceeds in the event of your death. Generally, there are better and less expensive ways for you to save than through a life insurance policy.

Often, a family will only obtain life insurance on the primary breadwinner. In order to provide the greatest possible opportunity for a surviving spouse to stay home full time to raise the children, it would be wise to purchase policies for both husband and wife. Otherwise, in the event of the sudden death of the homemaker, the wage earner would need to continue working full time, with the exhaustion and stresses that come with being a single parent.

Another key question is determining how much insurance you need. No one answer fits every situation. You'll want to take into account your ongoing expenses and future major expenditures, such as debt repayment, college tuition, or the purchase of a new car. By comparing these needs to your existing resources, you can better understand how much insurance is right for you. A general rule of thumb is to start with a figure of 10 times your ongoing expenses. The reason for this is that over an extended period of time, you should be able to achieve a 10 percent return on the insurance proceeds. The resulting return should be adequate to cover the cost of those needs without tapping in to the principal. The *7 Steps to Becoming Financially Free Workbook* provides a form to help you calculate your life insurance needs.

Disability Insurance

Disability insurance is an important form of coverage, especially given the fact that there is a higher probability that you'll experience a disability than die at an early age. Some employers offer group disability policies for their employees, and this can be a relatively inexpensive way to obtain some coverage. If your employer doesn't offer a group policy, you'll have to consider purchasing an individual policy. However, individual policies are quite expensive for the expected benefit. While they certainly make sense for professionals with higher incomes, especially those in the medical profession, it can be difficult for the average family to squeeze into the budget.

Here's how a basic plan works. You pay an annual premium in order to receive a fixed dollar amount of monthly income in the event you become disabled. The premium will primarily depend on your job classification and your age. Most policies will limit the amount of your benefit to no more than 60 percent of your income at the time of disability, but it may be prohibitively expensive for you to pay for full coverage. Because of the cost, many will need to accept a benefit quite a bit lower than the 60 percent upper limit. While I recommend that most families have at least a base level of disability insurance, I also understand that given the high cost, other priorities may be more important. Take the time to talk about the risks your family faces in the event of a disability and visit an insurance professional to see whether there is an option that's appropriate for you.

Remember that there are scores of companies that sell life and disability insurance. While price is certainly important, you'll also want to consider the financial strength of the company you're dealing with (look for a rating of A or better from A.M. Best, a company that rates the financial strength of insurance companies). As with any purchase, comparison shopping results in great savings. It would be a good idea to obtain a number of quotes before making a decision.

 FREEDOM DIVIDENDS

- Develop your own price book, listing those items that you purchase regularly.
- When making your next major purchase, work through the habits of the financially free: make sure it's part of your budget, consider "non-brand" items, comparison shop, consider buying it used, and sleep on it. You'll save money and make a better decision.

Chapter 11

SAVING AND INVESTING
WITH A PURPOSE

*A*s I developed the outline for the chapters on saving and investing, two primary objectives became clear. The first directly
relates to the title of this chapter: "Saving and Investing with
a Purpose." I want to answer the question "Why should we save?" and provide the Christian principles that should form our attitude toward saving
and investing.

My second objective is to offer practical guidelines to help you develop
a solid savings and investment strategy appropriate for your state in life.
While it's not within the scope of this book to recommend specific investments, it is important to explain what a basic plan looks like. Often, information on savings and investing is presented in such a technical manner
that it takes a Ph.D. to understand. I want to avoid the stilted language and
show you step-by-step how to map out an effective strategy for your future.
I'll be covering these issues in the next chapter, "Six Habits for Successful
Investors." I've also provided references to some of the most respected
materials on investing in Appendix B, so those interested in delving more
deeply into the topic can do so.

WHY SHOULD WE SAVE AND INVEST?

People often misinterpret the Scripture "For the love of money is the root
of all evils" (1 Tim 6:10) to mean that money itself is evil. They think of
profits and investing as somehow not the Christian way. That's not true.
Money is just an object that can be used for either good or bad. It's the *love*
of money and its misuse that are the problems. The Lord doesn't condemn

the multiplication of our assets. In fact, he instructed us to work for such an increase in the parable of the good steward (Mt 25:14–30). What's important is that we use these resources in a godly manner.

Why should we save? First of all, to meet our future needs. Let's consider the example of Joseph in the Old Testament book of Genesis (see Gen 41). You remember how he was the favorite son of his father, Jacob. Out of jealousy, his brothers sold him off to travelers headed to Egypt. While there, he became known for his wisdom and was able to interpret the pharaoh's dreams. In one of those dreams, pharaoh is forewarned about seven years of plenty to be followed by seven years of famine. He assigns Joseph the task of managing Egypt's affairs during this time so they will be prepared for the future. Joseph wisely set aside grain from the good years so there would be food available during the years of shortage. This is a classic example in Scripture of saving — putting aside resources from today's surplus to meet needs down the road.

What are examples of future requirements you should be saving for? They include your emergency fund; major purchases, such as a down payment on a home or paying cash for your next automobile; the education of your children; and your retirement. A second reason for saving and investing, beyond meeting your own needs, is to grow resources that you can invest in the lives of others.

SAVING AND INVESTING: TWO EXTREMES

When it comes to saving and investing, Americans largely fall into two camps. The vast majority fail to save at all, and as a result, experience the turmoil of living paycheck to paycheck, often relying on credit to make ends meet. When Alan Greenspan, the former Chairman of the Federal Reserve, testified before Congress in 2005, he said, "The sizable gains in consumer spending of recent years have been accompanied by a drop in the personal savings rate to an average of only one percent over 2004 — a very low figure relative to the nearly 7 percent rate averaged over the previous three decades." This low savings rate and the problems it creates reminds me of the proverb, "Precious treasure remains in a wise man's dwelling, but a foolish man devours it" (Prov 21:20).

For others, though, investing becomes a game, with the goal of acquiring as much personal wealth as possible. They play to "win." One of the most popular board games of all time is *Monopoly*. The objective of the game is to end up with the most money, and those who have played *Monopoly* will be familiar with the adrenalin rush that comes when you're able to purchase Boardwalk, Park Place, and the other valuable properties that lead to winning. *Monopoly* reminds me of the license-plate frame, "He who dies with the most toys wins." This attitude leads to narcissism and a sense of selfishness. In this case, Paul's words to Timothy should be heeded: "But those who desire to be rich fall into temptation, into a snare, into many senseless and hurtful desires that plunge men into ruin and destruction. For the love of money is the root of all evils; it is through this craving that some have wandered away from the faith and pierced their hearts with many pangs" (1 Tim 6:9–10).

LIFESTYLE DECISIONS: IMPACT ON SAVINGS AND SPIRITUAL HEALTH

I remember hearing the results of a survey awhile back, and although I don't recall all the particulars, the results intrigued me. People were asked how much they would need to earn annually in order to feel "rich." The answers went something like this: those who currently earned $50,000 per year would feel rich if they made $100,000, those who currently earned $100,000 felt they would be rich if they made $250,000, and so on. You get the picture. Even those who earned $1,000,000 annually felt they needed to make more to "feel rich." When asked how much more he would need to feel rich, Henry Ford is reported to have said, "Just a little bit more." This after he had already made a billion dollars!

The ability to save is certainly a function of how much income you earn. But at least as important is the lifestyle you choose and the spending that goes along with it. This is important on two fronts: First, Americans aren't saving adequately to meet their future needs, largely because of their lifestyle decisions; and second, these same decisions are sometimes harmful to their spiritual health. Answering the question "How much is enough?" is a challenge for most of us, especially in our consumer-driven society. Consider the words of St. Robert Bellarmine:

May you consider truly good whatever leads to your goal and truly evil whatever makes you fall away from it. Prosperity and adversity, wealth and poverty, health and sickness, honors and humiliations, life and death, in the mind of the wise man, are not to be sought for their own sake, nor avoided for their own sake. But if they contribute to the glory of God and your eternal happiness, then they are good and should be sought. If they detract from this, they are evil and must be avoided.[36]

If you have resources left over after meeting your basic needs, you'll want to use those resources to "do what is good and avoid what is evil" (CCC 1706). Doing good can take many forms, including additional spending on your own family and sharing your resources with others.

Let me share a few examples from our family. Some of our most treasured memories come from our family vacations. Once a year, we have a tradition of spending about 10 days in a cabin at one of several alpine lakes in California. It's a time for the family to relax and unwind after months of a harried schedule. We enjoy time on the lake, hiking, cycling, and eating plenty of ice cream!

We have also chosen to sponsor children through a missionary program. The funds help meet the current physical needs of these young people, but also provide for their education and help the community develop its economy so that they can become more self-sufficient. As the saying goes, "Give a man a fish and you feed him for a day; teach a man to fish, and you feed him for a lifetime."

As you consider how to use your resources, one attitude you'll want to avoid is hoarding. The Lord explicitly warns us against this in Luke 12:16–21. It reads:

And he told them a parable, saying, "The land of a rich man brought forth plentifully; and he thought to himself, 'What shall I do, for I have nowhere to store my crops?' And he said, 'I will do this: I will pull down my barns, and build larger ones; and there I will store all my grain and my goods. And I will say to my soul, Soul, you have ample goods laid up for many years; take your ease, eat, drink, be merry.' But God said to him, 'Fool! This night your soul is required of you; and the things you have prepared, whose will they be? So is he who lays up treasure for himself, and is not rich toward God.'"

A godly perspective on savings and investing recognizes the need to save for future obligations. But it also acknowledges that there is a limit to our needs, and calls us to live out the virtues of temperance and detachment. That's not to say that we're all called to the exact same lifestyle. But it does mean that once your valid needs have been met, you should avoid setting an ever higher standard of living when the resources could clearly serve a better purpose. Instead, we should recognize that our excess is able to help provide for others (see 2 Cor 8:13–15).

In a materialistic culture such as ours, it is difficult to be objective when making lifestyle decisions — especially if we have resources beyond our basic needs. Place this question of lifestyle in prayer with the "Counselor of Counselors." As we read in Isaiah, 9:6, "For to us a child is born, to us a son is given; and the government will be on his shoulder, and his name will be called 'Wonderful Counselor, Mighty God, Everlasting Father, Prince of Peace.'" Also consider the example of godly people you find worthy of imitation. Finally, seek counsel from those who are close to you. Your spouse, a good friend, or your spiritual director can help keep you on a solid foundation. Just as you would want them to let you know if you were drinking too much or not spending enough time with your family, so they can be a source of insight when it comes to lifestyle decisions and how you use your money. Keep in mind the wisdom of Proverbs 30:8–9, which says, "Give me neither poverty nor riches; feed me with the food that is needful for me, lest I be full, and deny thee, and say, 'Who is the LORD?' or lest I be poor, and steal, and profane the name of my God."

SETTING GODLY GOALS AND PRIORITIES

So how can we set godly goals and priorities when it comes to saving and investing? I touched on this in previous chapters, but I'll recap here:

- Set aside a $2,000 emergency fund.
- Start a rainy-day fund of six months' expenses.

- Begin saving for major purchases, such as automobiles or the down payment on a house.
- Prepay your mortgage.
- Plan the funding of your retirement.
- Assist with funding the formation and education of your children and grandchildren.
- Pass on a reasonable inheritance.
- Start tithing, which means giving to grow the Kingdom of God.

Early and Steady Make All the Difference — Compound Earnings

One of the greatest mathematical discoveries of all time — according to Einstein — is the "miracle" of compound interest. It will either be one of your greatest financial friends or one of your worst financial foes. Let me show you what I mean with two examples.

Let's consider how compound interest rewards those who save early and consistently by reviewing the following example of two couples. Paul and Ann save $2,000 per year for 10 years, starting when they're 25. While they stop making additional contributions after the first 10 years, they let the investment balance continue to grow at 10 percent until they are 65 years old. John and Carol, on the other hand, don't start saving until they're 35. They contribute $2,000 per year for 30 years, yet never catch up to Paul and Ann! This is the power of compound interest. Paul and Ann contributed $20,000, but did so early, and it grew to $677,000. John and Carol contributed $60,000, but since they started late, it only had time to grow to $377,000. Which couple would you rather be?

Now let's consider another example. According to the U.S. Census Bureau, the real median household income for 2004 was about $43,000. We previously saw that the average household carries $8,000 in credit card debt. Assuming an interest rate of 20 percent, households are paying about $1,600 per year — or between 3 and 4 percent of their income — in interest on just their credit cards. It's little wonder that the savings rate in America is so low. We're paying credit card companies and banks the money we used to save! What would happen if you eliminated the credit card debt and invested the $1,600 with a 10 percent annual return over 40 years? You

Year	Paul and Ann Savings	Paul and Ann Savings and Compound Interest	John and Carol Savings	John and Carol Savings and Compound Interest
25	2,000	2,094	0	0
26	2,000	4,407	0	0
27	2,000	6,963	0	0
28	2,000	9,787	0	0
29	2,000	12,906	0	0
30	2,000	16,352	0	0
31	2,000	20,159	0	0
32	2,000	24,364	0	0
33	2,000	29,010	0	0
34	2,000	34,142	0	0
35	0	37,717	2,000	2,094
36	0	41,666	2,000	4,407
37	0	46,029	2,000	6,963
38	0	50,849	2,000	9,787
39	0	56,173	2,000	12,906
40	0	62,055	2,000	16,352
41	0	68,553	2,000	20,159
42	0	75,732	2,000	24,364
43	0	83,662	2,000	29,010
44	0	92,422	2,000	34,142
45	0	102,100	2,000	39,811
46	0	112,792	2,000	46,074
47	0	124,602	2,000	52,993
48	0	137,650	2,000	60,636
49	0	152,064	2,000	69,080
50	0	167,987	2,000	78,408
51	0	185,577	2,000	88,712
52	0	205,009	2,000	100,096
53	0	226,476	2,000	112,672
54	0	250,192	2,000	126,564
55	0	276,390	2,000	141,911
56	0	305,331	2,000	158,865
57	0	337,304	2,000	177,595
58	0	372,624	2,000	198,286
59	0	411,642	2,000	221,143
60	0	454,747	2,000	246,394
61	0	502,365	2,000	274,289
62	0	554,969	2,000	305,105
63	0	613,081	2,000	339,148
64	0	677,279	2,000	376,756
Total	20,000	677,279	60,000	376,756

would have a balance of $843,000, rather than having paid the bank $64,000!

Saving and investing early and consistently over an extended period of time will revolutionize your financial life and help you reach the goals you have for yourself and your family. One of the keys to succeeding is to not allow your savings to be swallowed up with payments on credit cards.

Living Below Your Means Today So You Can Meet Your Needs Tomorrow

Let me give you another important hint when it comes to saving. You'll need to make your savings preplanned, just like your giving, otherwise it won't happen. Again, you'll find that your money grows legs and walks away. By planning your saving as part of your budget, you set a lifestyle below your means today so you'll have resources for tomorrow's needs. This is called *delayed gratification* and it's the only way you'll reach financial freedom.

Generally speaking, a good rule of thumb is to save between 10 to 15 percent of your gross income. Once you've budgeted for savings, use direct deposit as the way to make sure it gets into the savings account. You won't miss the funds and it makes your saving automatic. Think of the peace you'll have when you can pay cash for the next "emergency" or your next car, or help your child obtain a college education, and then retire secure with the knowledge that you have the resources you'll need during your later years.

Emergency Fund and Saving for Major Purchases

I've already discussed setting aside emergency funds in Chapter 7, but it's worth recapping here. This is your first savings priority. Your initial goal is to set aside $2,000, because until you do, you'll never be able to break free from the habit of paying for "emergencies" by using credit cards. After you've saved your $2,000, you'll want to eliminate any credit card debt by following the steps in Chapter 8. Once your credit card debts are eliminated, you'll want to set up a rainy-day fund until six months' living expenses are safely set aside.

Your next step is to save up for major purchases, such as a down payment on a home or cash for your next automobile. Money you put away for your emergency fund and for major purchases are short-term savings and should not be commingled with your long-term investments. You will be expecting to need these funds within five years. As a result, you'll want to place them in accessible places. You can keep three months savings in a money-market type account that has check-writing privileges with a bank or brokerage house, and place the remainder in a three-month Certificate of Deposit in order to enhance your overall return.

Funding Retirement

The need to save for retirement should be obvious. There will come a day for most of us when we're no longer able to earn a salary. Therefore, it's important during our earning years to plan for ongoing financial needs during that time.

There has been a lot of talk about Social Security over the last several years. It should be no surprise that Social Security will be providing less in benefits to future retirees than it does today. There just aren't enough young people entering the workforce to make up for all the baby boomers entering their retirement years. The message to take home is that you need to develop an appropriate savings strategy to fund your own retirement needs.

While your circumstances will be unique, a typical rule of thumb is that you will need 80 percent of your pre-retirement income to meet your retirement needs. Some of your expenses, like housing and transportation, should decline substantially, but those are often largely offset by increasing medical and long-term care costs.

I'd like to make another point about retirement beyond the need to save for it. The broader culture seems to set a goal of "early and rich" retirement for people. You've seen the advertisements that show a carefree lifestyle on the beach. This attitude fails to recognize that work is a gift from God, and that how we go about doing the work God has called us to plays a substantial role in our sanctification. You know the saying, "All work and no play makes Jack a dull boy." The reverse is also true, in that all play and no work can make for an empty life.

One of the benefits of reaching true financial freedom is the ability it gives you to be more directly involved with God's work. Whether it's teaching in an inner-city school, building housing for the poor, working with the handicapped, becoming a deacon, or volunteering as a catechist at your parish, these all become options when you've saved for the future and avoided debt. So rather than retiring "early and rich," focus on how you can use the talents the Lord has given you in ways that glorify him and help make the world a better place. Give meaning to your life by investing in the lives of others.

The *7 Steps to Becoming Financially Free Workbook* provides further information on how you can develop a plan to fund your retirement years.

Giving to Grow the Kingdom of God

People who are blessed financially have been given a tremendous obligation. Once your needs have been met, this includes growing in generosity beyond the principle of the tithe. This is why it's so important to set a lifestyle that's reasonable in light of Christian teaching. We read in 2 Corinthians 8:13–14, "I do not mean that others should be eased and you burdened, but that as a matter of equality your abundance at the present time should supply their want, so that their abundance may supply your want, that there may be equality."

I remember the story about the founder of one of the companies I worked for. He and his wife had been successful at starting a business shortly after World War II that manufactured small trailers for people to live in. The initial success led them to seek capital for growth through a public stock offering. At the same time, the founder and his wife attended a small church that worshipped in temporary facilities. There were plans to build a church, but those plans would have to wait for the necessary funds. The stock offering was a success and the couple called the pastor to let him know they wanted to fund the building of the church. Over the years, this man and his wife continued to give very generously for a variety of needs. I remember hearing him once say that deciding where their donations should go was consistently one of the most difficult financial decisions he and his wife had to make. Wouldn't it be great if everyone took their call to generosity so seriously?

We have been given so much in America — opportunities that most of the world can only dream of. Think of giving as a privilege rather than a duty. You can make a big difference in the lives of those not so blessed and leave a legacy that will serve as an example for others to emulate. Isn't this an inheritance that should be considered as well as leaving an estate to your family?

FREEDOM DIVIDENDS

- Take time to consider "How much is enough?" for your life's circumstances. Place the question in prayer and discuss it with your spouse. Ask for the Lord's help in guiding you to a lifestyle that meets your needs and honors Him. Avoid the *Monopoly* syndrome and learn the joy of using your surplus for God's work.
- Complete the worksheets in the *7 Steps to Becoming Financially Free Workbook* related to housing, college savings, and retirement savings. Build these savings into your financial plan.

Chapter 12

SIX HABITS FOR SUCCESSFUL INVESTING

*H*ow can you develop an investment plan that will grow your savings and provide the resources you need for the future? As I mentioned in the last chapter, it's not the purpose of this book to provide advice about specific investments. Rather, I want to give you the time-tested principles that make up a solid investment plan. For those who would like to delve more deeply into this topic, I have provided a number of references in Appendix B.

#1 — SET CLEAR OBJECTIVES

Your first step in creating a successful investment plan is to understand your goals and objectives. You'll need to answer the question, "What am I saving for?" For example, you might set a goal of funding your retirement and paying for half the cost of your children's education. To determine what steps you should take today to accomplish these goals, you'll need to answer a few more questions:

- How much money will be needed in the future (factoring in inflation) to fund the goals you've set?
- What's a reasonable rate of return you can expect to earn on your investments?
- How long do you have to save before you'll need to tap in to the savings for each of your goals?

Once you've answered these questions, it becomes possible to estimate the amount you'll need to save and invest each month so you'll have the money needed at the appropriate time. The *7 Steps to Becoming Financially Free Workbook* provides examples that will help you apply these steps to your own situation.

#2 — UNDERSTAND YOUR INVESTMENTS: KEEP IT SIMPLE

The second investing principle is to understand what you're investing in. Today's investment world offers a wide range of opportunities. Some of these are straightforward and easily understandable, while others come with a high level of complexity. For some reason, when it comes to investing, people tend to get involved with things they don't understand. I'm sure this has to do with the "promise" of making killer returns, yet it's also a good way to lose bundles of money.

For most of us who are focused on raising families and working to make ends meet, we have a limited amount of time to spend on learning about and being actively engaged with the investment world. While it's important for everyone to have a basic understanding, unless you plan on becoming a very active investor and have the time to do so, you'll want to develop a more simple strategy. The good news is that with the tools available today, it is much easier to succeed with your investment objectives than it has been in the past.

Mutual Funds

Unless you use the services of a trusted investment professional or have loads of time and the interest to do your own research, I wouldn't recommend investing in individual stocks and bonds. A more effective approach for the average investor is to purchase stocks as part of a mutual fund. The concept behind a mutual fund is very simple: People pool their money together under the management of a professional, called a "fund manager," who then uses the money to purchase a number of different stocks.

There are many benefits to owning mutual funds. They provide for diversification, a principle found in Ecclesiastes 11:2. Diversification simply means not putting all your eggs in one basket — or in this case, not putting all of your money into one stock. It's always possible for a single stock to suffer from unforeseen negative results, and it wouldn't be wise to have all of your savings tied up in one place. Just consider those who lost so much with the Enron and WorldCom debacles.

There are literally thousands of mutual funds available, which makes the selection process a bit difficult. But there are tools available to help you select and monitor the progress of funds that are appropriate for you. In fact, you'll find that there are mutual funds for just about every stage of your investing life. Most investment firms offer these funds according to a few broad risk and type categories, such as *aggressive* or *growth, moderate, conservative,* and *international.*

The aggressive funds typically seek to own stock in companies that will grow at above-average rates. These are often smaller companies that have a promising product. The more conservative funds will often purchase the stock of larger companies that have proven track records and can be counted on for more consistent results. The goal of the more conservative funds is to provide a reasonable return at a lower level of risk than the more aggressive funds. As you would expect, moderate funds fall between these two from a risk perspective. International funds allow you to invest in stocks of businesses outside the United States, including those of emerging economies, where higher growth rates are expected, although with a higher risk level.

This touches on an important subject for investors: the relationship between risk and rate of return. To the extent that investors accept a higher level of risk with an investment, they expect to earn a higher return. It's important for you to understand this principle and to develop a sense as to what your risk-tolerance level is. It's not unusual for a husband to be open to taking higher levels of risk than his wife (or vice versa), and sometimes this is a good thing, because you'll need to accept some risk over your investing lifetime if you want to achieve your goals. At the same time, some people have a tendency to "let it roll" and may fall into the trap of trying to get rich quick, making some very poor decisions in the process. In these cases, the more conservative spouse (in my experience, this is usually the wife) can bring proper balance to the situation. Take the time to share your perspectives on risk tolerance with each other. You'll find that it helps you achieve a more appropriate investment mix for your circumstances.

Most investment advisers will suggest that people allocate their savings into fund categories based on how long they can invest the money and not need to tap in to it. The longer the funds have to grow, the higher the allocation can be toward growth or higher-risk investments. If the time frame is relatively short (5 to 10 years), most advisers will suggest a more conservative allocation to limit the possibility of a sharp decline in your investments just as you may need to cash them out.

If you're more comfortable with conservative ventures, an important point to remember is the impact that inflation has on the long-term value of your investments. If inflation is running at 3 percent annually and you have all your money in certificates of deposit (CDs) earning an average of 4 percent, you're losing ground, especially after taxes. It's important that your overall investment strategy and risk tolerance takes into account the negative impact of inflation. Again, a reasonable long-term rate of return in the stock market is 10 percent, and you'll need to accept moderate levels of risk to achieve this rate of return.

Real Estate

For many, the family home may end up being one of their largest assets. It's a great way to be invested in real estate as well. But beyond home ownership is the opportunity to invest in rental property. Good friends of my parents began investing in real estate in the 1950s. They started slow and purchased a duplex as their first home. The rent they received covered the cost of their total payment, so they were able to save money to eventually purchase a single family home. Over the years, they were successful at obtaining and managing many additional properties that have performed very well for them.

Many real estate investors rely heavily on debt to finance the purchase of their properties. As a result, especially during the early years of ownership, they are at high risk of default if the local market experiences major price and rent declines. If you have an interest in investing in real estate, start small and minimize the level of debt you're taking on. Make sure the debt is secured only by the related property and *not* your personal residence or other investments. In addition, it's wise to have an adequate cash cushion so you know that you can weather any economic downturn. Also remember that real estate is historically a cyclical investment — some people have lost everything because they were overly aggressive with the use of debt to acquire properties they really couldn't afford.

One final note on the subject: It's important that you factor in the total cost of ownership, including the amount of time that this type of investment can take from your family life. Real estate can be a great way to make money, but go into it with your eyes wide open.

#3 — REGULARLY MONITOR YOUR INVESTMENT PORTFOLIO

Before you select funds to invest in, you'll want to understand their past performance. While it's no guarantee of how the fund will perform in the future, it's an important step in the selection process. Then, once you've begun investing, it becomes crucial to track how your portfolio is performing. The website www.Morningstar.com offers an array of free tools that allow you to accomplish both of these objectives by monitoring the most important factors related to your investments. I recommend keeping track of at least the following:

- The rate of return over 4 periods of time: year to date, 3-year, 5-year, and 10-year.
- The name of the fund manager and his tenure with the fund — you're looking for stability at the management position.
- Expense ratio: While it's certainly good to have a low expense ratio, greater emphasis should be on net return.
- Stock index results for indexes comparable to your fund. Examples include the S & P index for large cap (large company) funds, the Russell 2000 index for small cap (small company) funds, and the MSCI EAFE index for international funds. By comparing your fund's results to these benchmarks, you can see if it's performing at a reasonable level.

Fortunately, Morningstar automates this process, so all you need to do is know the "ticker symbol" of your investments. If you're the average investor who is steadily saving and investing in mutual funds, but isn't truly active, quarterly reviews of your funds' performance should be adequate. You're in it for the long haul, and are primarily interested in knowing that your funds are performing at least on par with the primary indexes they're compared to. Again, the Morningstar site can help make this very easy as it allows you to track data on up to 50 stocks/funds in one portfolio. If you find that you own certain funds that are consistently underperforming, sell them and reinvest in better performing ones. (Before you do so, check with your tax adviser regarding the tax consequences of selling your investments.)

#4 — LOOK FOR TAX-FAVORED INVESTMENTS

Tax Incentives for Higher Education

The federal government provides special tax incentives to help fund higher education costs. These incentives come in the form of tax deductions for certain education expenses and tax-favored savings plans, which allow your investments to grow tax free. As you would expect with tax-related issues, each of these benefits comes with its own complex set of rules, so you'll want to consult a professional adviser about how you can take advantage of them. I won't go into a detailed explanation of these tools, but here is a brief summary (find a more complete explanation at http://www.irs.gov/pub/irs-pdf/p970.pdf).

There are two types of tax credits related to higher education. The first is the HOPE scholarship credit, which allows taxpayers to take a credit of up to $1,500 per student per year for qualified tuition and fees paid for the first two years of qualified higher education expenses. The second deduction is the Lifetime Learning Credit, which allows a credit of up to 20 percent of qualified tuition and fees paid on behalf of the taxpayer, his spouse, or dependents. You have the option of using one or the other of these credits, but not both for the same expenses.

There are also two types of tax-favored savings plans available for higher education (post-secondary). The first is the Coverdell Education Savings Account, which allows you to save up to $2,000 per year per beneficiary. While there is no deduction for the initial contribution, the earnings grow tax free if used for qualified expenses.

Finally, qualified state tuition programs, more commonly known as 529 plans, offer a way to set aside a higher level of savings than the $2,000 per year allowed by the Education Savings Accounts. You'll probably want to start by funding the Education Savings Accounts since you'll have more flexibility with how the investments are managed.

Tax Incentives for Retirement

The government also offers incentives for individuals to save for retirement, whether employed by a company that offers a retirement plan or not. If you work for a company that offers a 401k or 403b savings plan, by all means, take advantage of it, especially if they offer to match a portion of your savings. That's like getting a 100 percent return! Even if your employer offers no plan, the government allows individuals to save for retirement via standard Individual Retirement Accounts (IRAs) and Roth IRAs, which allow you to save several thousand dollars per year and receive tax-favored treatment. The primary difference between the two IRAs is that the standard IRA allows a deduction from current income and earnings to grow tax deferred. Taxes are paid on the contributions and earnings when the money is withdrawn at retirement. The Roth, on the other hand, doesn't allow for a current deduction, but the earnings grow completely tax free.

Many financial planners lean toward the Roth IRA as the better option for most people, although it truly depends on a number of factors, including the following:

- Your marginal tax rates at the time of contribution and the expected rate at the time of distribution.
- How long the account can grow before the money will be distributed. (The longer the time period, the better the Roth account is.)

In addition to the typical 401k plans sponsored by many employers, the government also offers an array of options for small business owners when it comes to retirement plans. If you are a small business owner, check with your accountant to better understand your options.

#5 — APPLYING MORAL CRITERIA TO INVESTMENT DECISIONS

I am frequently asked about what level of responsibility we have as Catholics to take moral criteria into account with our investment dollars. How should we view investing in a large conglomerate that on the one hand produces a number of good products, but on the other hand makes an annual donation to Planned Parenthood? Or a large drug manufacturer that does a great deal of good, but also manufactures a birth control pill that acts as an abortifacient?

Pope John Paul II wrote, "Even the decision to invest in one place rather than another, is always a *moral and cultural choice.*"[37] We certainly want to "do what is good and avoid what is evil"[38] in our investment decisions, but because the economy is so complex, it can be difficult to draw black and white lines. Concerned Catholics typically need to answer whether their investing in a company creates a level of cooperation that is problematic. In the vast majority of cases, the cooperation ends up being of a very limited nature. The company is typically involved in a number of positive areas, but may have a product line or make certain donations that are deemed immoral. Because the concerned Catholic doesn't share the goal of the company when it comes to those areas, there is no formal cooperation. The actual investment does involve a certain level of material cooperation, but this needs to be looked at in light of the magnitude of the investment. In the typical scenario, the investment represents a very small fraction of the company's funding, and the investor has a very limited ability to influence its decisions. Because of this, any cooperation tends to be remote in nature, and accordingly, investing in such companies is not disallowed.

At the same time, it would be a good thing to be able to invest solely in companies that promote the good, and that is becoming easier today. There are several mutual funds that are available that screen their investments to exclude companies that have problematic activities. While not obligated to use them, to the extent that these funds are able to offer the same benefits to the Catholic investor that secular funds do, they are certainly worth considering as part of your investment portfolio.

#6 — AVOID GET-RICH-QUICK SCHEMES

One of the sad aspects of investment scams is that frequently those who can least afford to lose the money find themselves victims of a fraud. I just received a letter from one family who fell into this trap. Their financial situation had been tight for some time, with growing credit card bills, when the wife heard about an opportunity for a home-based business that would allow her to stay home with their children while generating sufficient income to pay down their debts. In order to get started in the business, a $12,000 fee was required, plus equipment and training to the tune of another $4,000. Since the couple had no savings, these charges also went on credit cards.

You can guess what happened. After taking the money from who knows how many people, the operators are nowhere to be found. Now this family, who already had credit card problems, is in the position of having added thousands of dollars more to their debt.

How can you avoid making a costly mistake such as this one? The following principles in the Bible will help you avoid investment scams. First, don't fall into the trap of seeking quick riches. In Proverbs 13:11, we read, "Wealth hastily gotten will dwindle, but he who gathers little by little will increase it." Take time to adequately research any investment before you hand over funds. Proverbs 21:5 says, "The plans of the diligent lead surely to abundance, but everyone who is hasty comes only to want." In other words, if it sounds too good to be true, it probably is! Of equal importance to solid research is seeking good counsel, especially from your spouse. And don't borrow money to invest unless there is a guaranteed method of repayment. If you'll be relying on the value of the investment to pay back the debt, remember Proverbs 27:1, which warns, "Do not boast about tomorrow, for you do not know what a day may bring forth."

A Word about Gambling

Using the excuse that they simply want to "live life to its fullest," people often experiment with behaviors that, in reality, have nothing to do with living a full life, but rather, a life of bondage. These behaviors include drug and alcohol abuse, sexual activity outside of the marriage covenant, and one that I would add to the list: compulsive gambling.

Let me share a true story with you about a married couple, Ed and Sue. A number of years ago, Ed lived in a state where gambling was legal, and he was itching to play the slot machines when he turned 21. It started innocently enough, but as time passed he felt the need to keep going back to the casino. After several years of marriage and parenthood, he found it added an excitement to his life that he otherwise believed was missing.

He didn't realize that he had become addicted to gambling. Ed found himself lying to his wife and co-workers about how he was spending his time. Since he was handling the family finances, he also had to lie to his wife about where their money was going. He made a good income, yet even that wasn't enough to feed his habit. So in order to keep gambling, he accepted one credit card after another, relying on advances from new accounts to meet his minimum payments on the older ones. In the end, Ed had amassed $140,000 in debt on 28 credit cards!

But it didn't stop there. As a trusted financial officer, he embezzled another $360,000 from his employer. It all came crashing down when Ed finally realized how far in over his head he was. In desperation, he even became suicidal. Thanks be to God, he sought help at a Catholic hospital, and ever so slowly he and Sue have rebuilt their life together. But on the way, they have had to declare bankruptcy, and Ed spent some time in prison after being convicted of embezzlement.

You may say this will never happen to you, but I guarantee, Ed and Sue never thought it would happen to them, either. It's true — the Church doesn't consider games of chance in themselves to be contrary to justice. Yet the *Catechism of the Catholic Church* says, "They become morally unacceptable when they deprive someone of what is necessary to provide for his needs and those of others. The passion for gambling risks becoming an enslavement" (CCC 2413).

Gambling has proliferated over the last two decades, with expansions of state lotteries and Indian casinos. The National Gambling Impact Study Commission's report, which was released in 1999, noted that in 1989, gambling was legal in only two states. By 1999, it was legal in 48 states, causing much wider devastation than ever before on the family. I encourage you to avoid the dangers associated with gambling and seek a more wholesome form of entertainment and recreation.

FREEDOM DIVIDENDS

- Have a "family budget meeting" to discuss your investment goals. Answer the question what you need to save for, and use the *7 Steps to Becoming Financially Free Workbook* to develop a specific plan.
- Set up a system to monitor your investments on a quarterly basis. See the sample schedule in the *7 Steps to Becoming Financially Free Workbook*.

Epilogue

*I*t has been a pleasure for me to be a partner with you on this journey to true financial freedom. At no matter what stage you are on this journey, remember that it is a lifelong endeavor for all of us. Maybe you're a young adult just getting underway with your financial responsibilities and want to get started on the right track. Or maybe you are further along in this journey of life and need to make a few corrections along the way. Or maybe you are somewhere in between. It is my hope that as you apply the tools you've been equipped with in *7 Steps to Becoming Financially Free*, you'll develop a deeper walk with the Lord, become a "Steward of Providence," and effectively fulfill the responsibilities the Lord has entrusted to you. May God bless you.

7 STEPS TO BECOMING FINANCIALLY FREE

 STEP ONE Be a "Steward of Providence"

 STEP TWO Assess Where You Are – Develop a Plan

 STEP THREE $2,000 Emergency Savings

 STEP FOUR Eliminate Debt – Accelerate It!

 STEP FIVE Rainy-Day Fund – Six Months' Expenses

 STEP SIX Review Insurance and Estate Planning Needs

 STEP SEVEN Save and Invest with a Purpose

PRAYERS

A MORNING OFFERING

O Jesus, through the Immaculate Heart of Mary, I offer you all my prayers, works, joys, and sufferings of this day, for all the intentions of your Sacred Heart, in union with the Holy Sacrifice of the Mass throughout the world, in thanksgiving for your favors, in reparation for my sins, for the intentions of all my relatives and friends, and in particular for the intentions of the Holy Father. Amen.

PRAYER TO THE HOLY SPIRIT

Come Holy Spirit, fill the hearts of your faithful and enkindle in them the fire of your love.

> **V.** Send forth your Spirit and they shall be created;
> **R.** And you shall renew the face of the earth.

Let us pray:
O God, who did instruct the hearts of the faithful by the light of the Holy Spirit, grant us in the same spirit to be truly wise, and ever to rejoice in his consolation. Through Christ our Lord. Amen.

Follow these prayers with your morning spiritual reading.

THE ANGELUS

V. The Angel of the Lord declared unto Mary;
R. And she conceived of the Holy Spirit.

Hail Mary, full of grace, the Lord is with you, blessed are you among women and blessed is the fruit of your womb, Jesus. Holy Mary, Mother of God, pray for us sinners, now and at the hour of our death. Amen.

V. Behold the handmaid of the Lord.
R. Be it done unto me according to your word.

Hail Mary . . .

V. And the Word was made flesh,
R. And dwelt among us.

Hail Mary . . .

V. Pray for us, O holy Mother of God,
R. That we may be made worthy of the promises of Christ.

Let us pray:
Pour forth we beseech you, O Lord, your grace into our hearts, that we to whom the incarnation of Christ, your Son, was made known by the message of an angel, may by his passion and cross be brought to the glory of his resurrection, through the same Christ our Lord.

R. Amen.

Appendix B

ADDITIONAL RESOURCES

WEBSITES

www.osv.com
www.VeritasFinancialMinistries.com

BOOKS

Griswold, Robert S., and Tyson, Eric. *Real Estate Investing for Dummies.* Hoboken, NJ: Wiley Publishing, Inc., 2004.

Hungelmann, Jack. *Insurance for Dummies.* Hoboken, NJ: Wiley Publishing, Inc., 2001.

Nissenbaum, Martin; Raasch, Barbara J.; and Ratner, Charles L. *Ernst & Young's Personal Financial Planning Guide, Fifth Edition.* Hoboken, NJ: John Wiley & Sons, Inc., 2004.

Tyson, Eric. *Investing for Dummies, 4th Edition.* Hoboken, NJ: Wiley Publishing, Inc., 2005.

Tyson, Eric. *Personal Finance for Dummies, 4th Edition.* New York: Wiley Publishing, Inc., 2003.

ARTICLES

Akin, Jimmy. "Moral Investing." *This Rock*, November 2005, 38.

Notes

1. Business Week: April 25, 2005, and the Gallup Organization: April 16, 2004.
2. Business Week: April 25, 2005.
3. www.uscourts.gov.
4. The Gallup Organization: May 18, 2004.
5. Independent Sector; The Barna Group: 2000.
6. The Barna Group: 1997.
7. http://www.family.org/cforum/fosi/marriage/divorce/a0037056.cfm; http://family-topics.custhelp.com/cgi-bin/family_topics.cfg/php/enduser/std_adp.php?p_faqid=1173.
8. *Catechism of the Catholic Church*, 1022.
9. Ibid., 2013.
10. Ibid., 2015.
11. Cf. ibid., 1709.
12. Ibid., 459.
13. Ibid.
14. Ibid., 2402.
15. Ibid., 2403–2404, emphasis added.
16. *Gaudium et spes*, n. 33, Vatican website (www.vatican.va).
17. *Catechism of the Catholic Church*, 2536.
18. Ibid., 1104.
19. Ibid., 1113.
20. Ibid., 2559.
21. Ibid., 1601.
22. Ibid., 1641.
23. Ibid., 1666.
24. Ibid., 1606.
25. Ibid., 1607.
26. Nielsen Survey, September 2005.
27. Ibid., September 2005.

[28] Nickelodeon U.S. Multicultural Kids Study, 2005.

[29] The average American Catholic gives about one percent.

[30] The tithing model proposes 10 percent.

[31] The tithe (10 percent) is a guideline. Those on low incomes should strive to be generous, but understandably may use more of their resources to meet basic needs. Those with higher incomes may find that 10 percent is not enough.

[32] Tax percentages are dependent on a number of factors, including the number of children in your family. Review your previous tax returns or consult a tax professional.

[33] Assumes part of tithe used for Catholic school tuition or homeschool expenses.

[34] This category includes saving for college and retirement. You should take into account any retirement program benefits from work (401k; pension) when determining your needs for this category.

[35] Veronis Suhler Stevenson: 19th Annual Communications Industry Forecast.

[36] Divine Office — Office of Readings, September 17: From a treatise on the ascent of the mind to God.

[37] *Centessimus Annus.*

[38] *Catechism of the Catholic Church,* 1706.